'When I first met Gilana
determined, pioneering visi
the suffering and appalling a
her short life or that God w
ahead through many further
cry, be inspired and, above all, allow God to speak to you
through Gilana's journey which is told with extraordinary
honesty. Be reminded that God has a purpose behind
suffering and uses circumstances to develop our character
and a deeper relationship with Him.'
Richard Wallis, Founder and CEO of Mission Possible

'If you are exploring your calling and think your back
story is getting in the way, this is a must-read. A gentle
and honest reflection on the inner and outer learning from
one woman's vocation. Courageous and vulnerable.'
Claire Pedrick, Managing Partner 3D Coaching

'This is a remarkable book. On the one hand it is a heart-
warming story of immense courage and persistence
matched by the immense graciousness of God, which has
brought the author to a place of wholeness and joyful
discipleship; on the other it is a book full of insight, advice
and encouragement both in what makes for spiritual
growth and what can be accomplished in ministry to those
who are broken. This is the candid and challenging tale of
a wounded healer who knows better than most that
healing is a lifelong process.'
*Rev Canon Michael Sansom, former Director of Ordinands, St
Albans Diocese*

'No one should be defined by a traumatic experience or traumatic periods in their lives. There is healing: no longer strangers or aliens, but citizens with the saints and members of the household of God (Ephesians 2:19). This is powerfully, beautifully and inspirationally illustrated in this transparent and honest book, which leaves the reader with hope and courage to engage in the healing process. A uniquely authentic account of the lived experience of childhood trauma, chronic illness and loss. It should be read by everyone who has been experiencing psychological trauma and illness, and also by those professionally involved with psychological trauma or illness, which is to say by all of us travelling on the journey of life. With compassion, Gilana takes us by the hand and shows us how to find meaning in suffering, making it touchingly clear that it is only by facing our fears through the grace of God and his unconditional love that we can start to hope and live again. An invitation to the banquet hall.'

Jannie van der Merwe, Consultant Psychologist

LED TO THE BANQUET HALL

Gilana Young

instant apostle

The views and opinions expressed in this work are those of the author and do not necessarily reflect the views and opinions of the publisher.

British Library Cataloguing-in-Publication Data

A catalogue record for this book is available from the British Library.

This book and all other Instant Apostle books are available from Instant Apostle:

Website: www.instantapostle.com

Email: info@instantapostle.com

ISBN 978-1-912726-30-1

Printed in Great Britain.

In loving memory
of my dearest
friend, Sue

Dear Andrew

Thank you for being
part of my story

Gill

Contents

Acknowledgements

I write this book in honour of my heavenly Father, my Lord Jesus and the Holy Spirit. I do so out of a profound sense of joy and gratitude for the relationship I enjoy with the Trinity.

Over a considerable number of years, I have had the privilege of spending time at several Christian retreat centres across the country. I am forever indebted to those precious places; namely St Cuthman's in Horsham, Burrswood in Tunbridge Wells (both disappointingly now closed), Harnhill Centre of Christian Healing in Cirencester, Launde Abbey in Leicester and especially Penhurst Retreat Centre, based near Battle in Hastings. They have all contributed to shaping the person I am today.

Two very special people have walked with me on what has at times felt like 'holy ground' through those inner encounters with God. My immense thanks go to Heather, my spiritual director, and to Judy, who has been my spiritual guide on several retreats, for listening, loving, inspiring and praying for me.

My heartfelt thanks to my friend and soulmate, Sue, who gently taught me how to love, to trust and to laugh; how I wish she was here to see the final outcome of this book.

God has provided many people to walk alongside me either for a season or for longer. Many of them have been His channels in offering love, support, acceptance and healing. I thank them hugely. Finally, thank you to Nicki and the team at Instant Apostle for encouraging me to persevere with writing this book!

Introduction

This book is a combination of sharing my personal life story and describing some of the work I have been privileged to be involved in. During the latter years, I have experienced the joys of taking time out to attend spiritual retreats, which have profoundly shaped my faith journey.

The title of the book, *Led to the Banquet Hall*, is based on the Song of Songs in the Old Testament. As God's children we are all invited into the most amazing 'place of banquet' that the verse from chapter 2 alludes to: 'Let him lead me to the banquet hall, and let his banner over me be love' (Song of Songs 2:4).

Many gifts can be bestowed upon us as we spend time at the banquet hall, in order to enhance our relationship with God and to equip us in our daily lives. It has taken me a long time to eat and drink from this inner sanctum in the way God has initiated and intended. Far too often I recognise how I have entered His sanctuary more as a 'beggar' within my own spirit, rather than taking on the mantle offered to me as a precious, invited child. As God has invited me to His banquet hall, He has generously offered me many gifts, which I have slowly but gratefully embraced. Throughout this book I share about some of these important bequests and the impact they have had on my life; namely, the gifts of being called, love, forgiveness, relationship, adoption, belonging, restoration, life and the gift of 'clothing'.

It is essential that all the individual gifts offered by God are grounded in biblical principles to equip us with a healthy, strong underpinning. That certainly helps when difficult emotions are being provoked. Solid foundations enable God's children to face those inner places of conflict and to hold on to His faithful assurances that He will never abandon us.

As with all major projects, this book has evolved from my original thoughts of purely sharing about going on spiritual retreats to what you are reading now. I had no intention of writing my life story – that's surely only for famous people – but God had other ideas! I hope through reading my narrative I may encourage others that God continually invites all of us to meet with Him at His banquet hall. We all have a choice about whether we believe He longs to share in our lives at a deeper level, or whether we decline that invitation.

Another reason for writing my book is I have reached the grand old age of sixty and I am also celebrating forty years of my Christian walk with God. I am humbled and so thankful at how God has remained faithful and understanding of all my frailties, which have needed His ongoing healing touch.

I have recently been diagnosed with Parkinson's disease, which has made me realise even more the importance of living 'today' and not holding back. One of the downsides to my Parkinson's is that I sometimes struggle to find the right words. I can miss words out when constructing sentences, so the very idea of writing a book makes me smile! It's another reminder that in my weaknesses I need to constantly lean on God's daily strength and wisdom as I endeavour to be 'His channel'.

Of course, one of the dangers of writing about personal experiences is that they can leave others feeling 'left out' if they fall into the trap of comparing their relationship with God to other people's. I know I have made the mistake of reading books that have left me downcast and despairing that I could never achieve what has been written about. We all have different make-ups (thank goodness!); no two life experiences are the same. My prayer is that this book encourages each of us to enter more and more into the banquet place God invites us to individually.

I acknowledge that God has done some amazing things in my life and I have rarely talked about them. A wise friend, on hearing my tentative thoughts concerning writing this book, encouraged me with the words, 'Your story might just help one other person.'

I have used a pseudonym to avoid any embarrassment or unnecessary hurt to my family. Gilana is the equivalent of my English first name in Hebrew and means 'eternal joy'.

Please be aware that the first chapter makes for grim reading, but it is an honest representation of the first eighteen years of my life, therefore it needs to be included.

1

A Relentless Nightmare

Imagine a married couple renting a two-bedroom terraced council house in the 1950s in a dilapidated neighbourhood, with five young children all under the age of six. The children's parents were holding down different jobs to bring in enough money for food and payment of bills. Dad was a telephone engineer and Mum worked in a 'pot bank' (a colloquial name for a pottery factory). At times they also took on cleaning jobs in the evenings.

In quick succession my parents had a son and a daughter and then, as their third child was born (at home), there was an announcement from the midwife, 'Hang on, another one is coming.' That 'other one' was me; unexpected and, as time was to demonstrate, not wanted. I became the scapegoat at an incredibly early age, in fact probably from birth, for all my parents' struggles and frustrations. Incredibly, my parents went on to have a fifth child, who was born eighteen months after my sister and me.

Without any exaggeration, I have no recollections of receiving any love, affection or nurture from my parents or any other adult. I have no memories of the early formative years of my life and can only recall a few incidents while attending the local infant school. On a regular basis, my mother ensured I was late to school by keeping me at home. I have no idea why she did that and can only conclude it was to ensure I was criticised and labelled as an 'undesirable' by the teachers. Fears and anxieties were constantly present inside me as I desperately tried not to be late by running the distance from home to school. No matter how fast I ran, I knew I wouldn't be successful, but I still tried!

I only have blurred memories of those early years and vaguely remember all five children sleeping in one room. As I try to recall the place there is a sense of it feeling very dark, intimidating and fearful – there was certainly no sense of it being a family home. I rarely spent any time with my siblings inside the house as I spent days, nights and weeks (during school holidays) isolated in cold, dark places of the house. I can remember spending long periods of time outside – sometimes playing with my siblings, but often on my own.

The back of the house led on to a pathway which many people used first thing in the morning to get to work or to a junior school. There were times when my mother would throw me outside with no clothes on, and you can imagine the embarrassment and fear I felt as a young child, desperately trying to find a place to hide so no one would see me as they walked past.

My parents' marriage was often stormy, with my mum repeatedly throwing accusations at my dad of having affairs (I have no idea if they were true or not). I vaguely hoped life would improve when my parents bought a three-bedroom house in a slightly better neighbourhood. Far from it: the relentless misery and abuse continued throughout the entire time I resided there. My 'bed' would consist of sleeping either in the bath or in the downstairs cloakroom, and sleep was often fitful as I was so cold (I have had sleep problems throughout my life, probably as a result of this). Physical violence was inflicted upon me at regular intervals. I ate 'meals' on my own which were appalling. Cold porridge with salt on it, bread soaked in water, raw eggs, cold meals coated with sugar.

Moving to a new neighbourhood coincided with the transition to junior school, and my mother escorted my younger brother, my twin and me part of the way before she went on to her place of work. Those journeys were a daily nightmare as my mother would wait until there were a lot of other people around us before shouting deeply personal insults at me. The few subjects I showed any promise in, my parents discouraged. I was picked to perform in school plays, which Mum and Dad allowed me to be part of, but on the actual performance nights they banned me from attending. It was awful having to go in to school the next day to face the repercussions of their actions. I loved to play hockey, but they refused to buy me the proper uniform; so, I was always the odd one out, and it became easier to stop playing. I probably had the intelligence to take O levels but my parents didn't engage with the regular open evenings where that kind of conversation could have been raised. Only one teacher saw potential in me and insisted I join his history O level class. I took CSEs for the rest of the subjects I studied.[1]

---

[1] A CSE (Certificate of Secondary Education) enabled children to leave school with an exam certificate, while the more able pupils took O level exams. This system was replaced in 1988 by

At times I feared for my life as I was subjected to endless cold baths, with my mother ducking me under the water until I was certain I would drown. I vividly recall the time she came close to strangling me.

In among all that misery, my bullying older brother sexually abused me with regular frequency. I was powerless to stop him, and being physically isolated from the rest of the household made me an easy target for him. I recall the unbearable tensions within me, fearing, as I became a teenager, that he might make me pregnant. I had no one I could talk to about these fears.

When all of this became too much, I would run away, even though as I escaped I knew it was futile. I had no money, my clothing was threadbare and there was nowhere to seek proper refuge. I would wander through different fields in the neighbourhood. My parents became familiar with the places I would go to, simply came and collected me and, of course, meted out more punishment.

The only relief came from the presence of the family dog, a Golden Labrador called Rufus. He meant a lot to me in the unspoken therapeutic ways that animals silently provide. The day I came home from school to discover he had been given away to my uncle because we lived near a main road, without any warning or discussion, switched another emotional light off inside me.

Turning sixteen and going to sixth-form college did make life more tolerable. I had been offered a place at the

---

the General Certificate of Secondary Education (GCSE). A Grade 1 CSE was deemed to be equivalent to an O level C grade.

college as I had gained grade ones in enough of my CSEs and had passed my history O level.

As I got older, I somehow managed to find ways to stand up to my parents when they were attempting to order my life in ways I knew would have an even more detrimental impact upon me. Attending college was one of those key moments. My father was insistent that both my twin and I had to do an apprentice-style job which would equip us with employment after the training. My twin went to do hairdressing at another local college (which she gave up as quickly as possible). I refused to acquiesce and, amazingly, they grudgingly accepted my standing up to them. However, as they were so against me continuing with my education, my parents made no attempt to encourage my studies. If I didn't have enough money from my Saturday job to catch the bus to college, I would walk the three and a half miles each way.

Life had also been eased by my parents having a sixth child, thirteen years after my younger brother, which was not planned (she was referred to as 'an accident' in the early years of her life). By this stage my parents were financially better off and my older brother and sister had left home, so there was more room in the house. My parents were more relaxed and enjoyed having their sixth child. They treated my younger sister almost as if she was their first child; they seemed to finally get what being a parent meant. A lot of the physical abuse towards me stopped as I was probably at that independent stage where they knew I could have reported them to the authorities.

Given my parents were so against me going to college, I vowed to prove them wrong, which was made more difficult with the reputation my older brother had gained while there. He had spent most of his time playing poker instead of attending lessons! I was constantly reminded of this fact by various teachers who had had the misfortune of trying to teach him and were now tutoring me. I took history and French A levels and Spanish O level, though the step up from CSE grade one in French to A-level standard was massive. I also had to juggle homework assignments while babysitting my younger sister, as my parents worked in the evenings and she would not go to sleep on her own. That meant having to physically stay with her in my parents' bed trying to get her to sleep, some nights for hours at a time.

I guess it was no surprise that when it came to the exams, my brain seemed to go on strike. I had endured so much emotional pressure and worked incredibly hard at trying to prove I was capable of undertaking A levels over those two years, there was mentally nothing left in me to combat the usual exam pressures. I struggled to find the necessary momentum to revise and was therefore surprised to gain one A level in history, albeit a low grade. I failed to gain the required grade for an A level in French but was awarded an equivalent O level grade.

I had no friends while at college, as I was too caught up in studying and babysitting. Boyfriends were few and, quite frankly, nightmarish. I didn't know how to relate to boys and struggled hugely when they wanted to get more intimate. My father would be so derogatory during those times I had a boyfriend that it simply wasn't worth listening to his tirades; it was easier not to bother.

I wanted to go into nursing after finishing college and was offered a place at Wolverhampton, but in those days there was a year's waiting list to get into a training college. I had been working in the food department of British Home Stores on Saturdays. This was in the days when food was all freshly produced and prepared on site. It was therefore a natural progression to go full-time with the aim of staying there while I waited my year out. Of course, this was frowned upon by my father; shop work was beneath his idea of suitable employment.

When British Home Stores offered me the opportunity to train as a manager, I jumped at the chance. This was despite an incident around my eighteenth birthday when my colleagues decided to take me to the pub at lunchtime. They encouraged me to drink vodka, which, of course, has little taste to it. After downing a few of those, we returned to work and I was heard singing upstairs in the food preparation area. My line manager was not impressed and, I belatedly realised, he could have sacked me. Instead, after a severe telling-off, he put me in one of the walk-in freezers to quickly sober up! I dread to think what he said to my colleagues, who he knew had led me astray.

Normally a management training course with British Home Stores involved spending a year going around every department within a store, but I was unusual in wanting to specialise in food management. The food training course was only for six months and involved being trained in a London store before being sent to Watford. As I was only eighteen, it was decided at head office level that I was too young to be in London on my own for the six months, so they paid for me to stay in a hotel in Ealing. Looking back, I can see God's hand in that unusual factor, as British Home Stores had never offered anyone else that kind of opportunity. I greatly valued their protection over me during that time as I was far too naïve and could easily have been overwhelmed with all that London offered.

I do not share these awful things about my early family life easily. I am not seeking to embarrass my family members, nor am I looking for revenge. Frankly, I would prefer not to divulge the levels of abuse I was subjected to, but it has been an essential part of my personal growth to own and embrace those first eighteen years of my existence. Far more importantly, the ultimate reason for disclosing them is to testify how God can turn the most horrendous events of our lives around with His transforming, compassionate grace, mercy and love. My hopes and prayers are that you will glean how He has achieved that in so many areas of my life in the ensuing chapters.

2
A Damaged Adult

You can probably imagine some of the pitfalls awaiting me during those six months I spent in a London hotel during my training course with British Home Stores! The hotel was a family-run one, so thankfully was quite small in terms of the number of occupants. I was very grateful and touched by how the staff took it upon themselves to 'look after' me. I remember one memorable occasion when they banned me from coming downstairs, as the hotel had been taken over by a rowdy group of rugby supporters! Instead, they brought food to my room and kept me out of harm's way.

During the time I was there, I became part of the small number of regular guests, predominantly male, who were resident during the weekdays and over the weekends. I was introduced to the drink Martini, and we would while away the evening hours creating the longest straw possible to drink with. I certainly learned how to use alcohol as a useful aid in numbing the memories of my past whenever they floated to the surface.

As I finally escaped the clutches of my dreadful family home, I mentally adopted a new identity. With every fibre of my being I cut off and disowned as much as was humanly possible all that had happened to me in those formative years of my life. As 'successful' as I was in this outward, ongoing survival mechanism, I struggled with many things most people take for granted in general day-to-day living.

It was no surprise to realise I had no concept of love or trust. I found it an incredibly difficult and sometimes torturous process to learn the skills I was having to absorb as an adult – skills that children in their developmental stages of growth spontaneously grasp. Attempting to form friendships was fraught, and being shown any kind of affection was deeply uncomfortable. I coped with day-to-day life by following a rigid rule of routine; I had no understanding of spontaneity. My sole ambition and achievement for many years was to work hard at my job. I possessed few decent outfits of clothing and initially I couldn't afford a new pair of shoes, so I had to wear some with holes in them. I felt awkward and very unsure of myself.

We know how events in our formative years shape our lives, and I recognise as I have got older how those abusive years had an impact on how I behaved as a young adult. It may seem astonishing to hear how I vowed very early on in my adult life never to marry or to have children, as a result of the abuse I had suffered. Even though I knew I would never abuse a child, I didn't want to ever put myself into a position of vulnerability, either with marriage or with bearing children.

As time went on, I understood many of my reactions and habits were linked with what had gone on in my childhood. Having an awareness helped on one level, but I seemed powerless to know how to overcome them, even though I desperately tried. I have always ensured I am never late for meetings and will usually be early. I became proficient at avoiding many activities which I knew would trigger flashbacks from my past – for instance, swimming.

I recognised I continued to repeat the patterns my parents had inflicted upon me as I struggled to see new things through – things I wanted to do, but quickly gave up on. One example of this was going to Ceroc dancing with a group of colleagues from work. I wanted to enjoy this social activity, but it became too much for me on an emotional level and I dropped out. Eating certain foods was a non-starter, and I struggled to be around big groups of people. I had to grit my teeth when I felt I had no choice but to conform and forced myself to endure those occasions.

I would remain silent and withdrawn when people shared about their early lives, their childhoods and their families. I feared if anyone discovered what my background had been like, I would be judged and found guilty and others would not want to know me any more. It was far safer to stay with the 'identity' I had adopted, even though there was little substance to it. Even to this day I rarely share details of my childhood, as it feels almost impossible to bring those awful memories into an ordinary conversation. I have often heard people describe me as being very private and didn't really understand what they meant by that. I now, of course, realise how little I let anyone in on the hidden side of who I am.

Internally, I recognised I was an emotionally empty shell. I had faced death so many times during my childhood from the numerous times my mother seemed to be trying to drown me and came very close to strangling me. For a long period I lived with the belief that I would be better off dead. There was little meaning to my existence, but that didn't mean I was in any way suicidal; it was more a reality of the emotional starkness within me. Life felt like a dirge; empty, with an enduring daily monotony, even though I was now able to live in freedom from emotional and physical abuse. I avoided being angry at all costs, to the point where I did not regard anger as an acceptable emotion. It took many years before I was able to shed tears and to feel OK about doing so.

I was nonplussed regarding how to relate to my brothers and sisters once I had left home, as there were too many unspoken secrets between us. There is often an assumption that siblings from large families relate well to each other and have a lot in common. That certainly wasn't the case with my family members; we were all totally different in our interests and life choices. Even my twin and I were poles apart. We had been put in different classes at school to 'encourage individuality', so there were none of the usual emotional ties that twins can have. For a long time, I avoided a deeper emotional connection with her.

I likened the first eighteen years of my life to that of someone who had been held in captivity as a hostage, even though they were totally innocent.

I may have been physically freed from that awful environment called 'home', but, unbeknown to me at the time, the hellish baggage that abuse forces you to carry internally continued to weigh heavily upon me. I recognised I was now outwardly free from all those years of imprisonment as a child, but inwardly I still felt locked away. In fact, many times it felt safer to stay confined to a prison cell within my own mind rather than to step outside and face a world with so much choice and opportunity.

It has taken me an incredibly long time to own the horrendous legacy inflicted upon me by my parents and brother, which included torture, poverty, relentless physical, mental, sexual and emotional abuse, nakedness, overwhelming fear, emptiness, abandonment, shame, hate, death and imprisonment.

3
Coming to Faith

After I had completed my six months of training in Ealing, British Home Stores transferred me to its store in Watford towards the latter end of 1978, which became home for me for the next twenty-eight years. About eighteen months into my time at the Watford store I was sent on a management course to Lindley Lodge, which was based in Nuneaton, Warwickshire (it is now a Youth With A Mission training base).

Indirectly, this event was to radically change my life. I have no recollection of how many people were on the course, but we were all split into groups and came under the direction of a trainer. During the week's programme, the trainer working with the group I was attached to was instrumental in changing the attitudes of young 'know-it-all' business-orientated people. We started to look out for each other and be supportive. We were all intrigued as to how the trainer had managed to achieve such transformations in a short space of time. The drastic change had only happened in our group, and others had noticed and were discussing it among themselves.

At our request, the trainer took the opportunity to share his Christian faith with the group on one of our free afternoons. As he talked, I sensed seeds of searching beginning to be sown within me. I mentioned to him that I was interested in hearing more about his faith. However, I hadn't banked on him phoning me up at regular intervals during work time, and I felt like I was being 'Bible bashed' during the next few months! In the end I decided the only way to stop the phone calls was to go on one of Lindley Lodge's exploring the Christian faith weekends.

So there I was, some months later, wondering what on earth would happen over this weekend. My boyfriend at the time drove me to Nuneaton and I was somewhat surprised when I was able to give him specific directions of where to go (anyone who knows me will be aware that this is an unusual feat!). Having driven me to Lindley Lodge on the Friday night, my boyfriend hotfooted it back to Watford, leaving me on my own with a couple I had never met before. I spent most of the Saturday making the couple work quite hard during our discussions of the merits of the Christian faith.

The gift of being called

What I hadn't expected was God's verbal intervention into the weekend. During the sleeping hours of Saturday night, I was awoken several times by my name being called. Each time I sat bolt upright in bed and then fell back to sleep. The next day, as I took the step of asking God into my life, I realised it had been God calling my name as I had been sleeping.

Even at that stage of my new-found faith, I was aware that this experience was unusual, and I wondered why it had occurred. As the years went by, I realised more and more the generosity of God in the way He spoke personally to me that Saturday night. I linked this experience with the words from the prophet Isaiah in the Old Testament, and they have always held a special place in my heart:

> But now, this is what the LORD says –
> he who created you, Jacob,
> he who formed you, Israel:
> 'Do not fear, for I have redeemed you;
> I have summoned you by name; you are mine.
> When you pass through the waters,
> I will be with you;
> and when you pass through the rivers,
> they will not sweep over you.
> When you walk through the fire,
> you will not be burned;
> the flames will not set you ablaze.
> For I am the LORD your God,
> the Holy One of Israel, your Saviour.'
> (Isaiah 43:1-3)

I have needed that solid reassurance of God calling me by name, and I have held on to the immense knowledge that I am His child. I am in no doubt that without the experience at Lindley Lodge my Christian walk would have been so much more difficult and probably, at times, impossible. God has drawn me back to these significant verses countless times during my journey and they have helped me to go deeper in my relationship.

I realise, as I write this book, that this was the first gift God generously offered me from His banquet place as described in Song of Songs 2:4. As God calls, so He invites all His children to join Him on an individual, lifetime journey of transformation at a pace He knows we can manage. He is far, far more patient with us than we probably are with ourselves. He will never force Himself on His people; He always waits to be invited. The journey we start with God is a wholehearted 100 per cent commitment on His side. God actively seeks, calls and invites each one of us into a personal relationship with Him.

The generous invitation is ongoing; it thankfully isn't a one-off encounter. There is something quite astonishing in the fact that God pursues us even when we mess up, which, of course, as human beings we will do, throughout our lives. If we go right back to the first book of the Bible, we see that Adam and Eve were created and initially enjoyed the utmost intimate relationship with God, but when they disobeyed Him, they became afraid and their natural inclination was to hide from His presence (see Genesis 3). It was God who went searching and calling for them. God knew what Adam and Eve had done when they were enticed to eat from the tree of forbidden fruit. He knew there would be consequences to their actions, but He didn't abandon them; He remained faithful in the relationship. When we think about it, this is quite awesome and deeply humbling.

When God calls us, He does so knowing all about our backgrounds, our personalities and what life experiences we have already gone through. God welcomes us just as we are; He doesn't wait until we have reached a place of 'being good enough' to invite us to have a relationship with Him.

We can choose to spend the rest of our life relating to God at a surface, mediocre, comfortable level, but that is not His wish. God's calling, His desire to relate to His children, is not about a thin, surface relationship. He invites us to connect with Him at a very deep level, and as we do so, He reciprocates. The gift of being called by God has an incredibly solid, foundational, biblical depth to it.

If you are wondering if that bequest includes you, I invite you to take some time to read Psalm 139, and hopefully, as you do so, you can grasp how God has been beckoning each one of us right from our conception.

I am convinced that God invited me to start a relationship with Him at a crucial time in my life when I could so easily have succumbed to many other unhealthy alternatives. I recognised my initial relationship with Him was at a 'mind' level, which was all I could cope with. God also knew that I needed to abide by a set of good rules, which becoming a Christian gave me, not only in the very early days of my relationship with Him but also for many years after.

I returned to Watford from the weekend at Lindley Lodge excited at my newly found faith, and shared my experience with two of my working colleagues who I knew were Christians. Interestingly, I lived next door to the local Baptist church; it therefore seemed a natural progression to attend the services there. Despite having been christened as a child, I immediately took on board the biblical exhortation from Mark's Gospel that, 'Whoever believes and is baptised will be saved' (Mark 16:16). I demanded to be part of the next scheduled adult baptism group, even though others were encouraging me to take my time.

On hearing the news about my faith, my parents ordered me home to explain what was going on. They thought I had joined a sect, and my mother's only comment to me was, 'Why don't you become a nun?'

Unsurprisingly, none of my family attended my adult baptism service. Publicly putting my trust in Jesus and testifying to how I had come to faith was an awesome experience. There was something profoundly important about the physical act of being fully immersed in water as a powerful symbol of confessing and repenting of my sins and knowing they were physically being washed away. There was also an underlying element of healing in this immersion in comparison with the many times I had feared being drowned by my mother's actions when I was subjected to cold baths. Adult baptism was a solid foundational stone for me in those early years as a young Christian and personally meant a great deal to me.

I cannot say my growth as a Christian was a smooth journey. People seemed to struggle to know how to encourage me and I was left very much to my own devices. I worked ridiculously long hours in my role as a food manager with British Home Stores. I would often be at work by five o'clock in the morning as there were not enough staff over the age of eighteen to handle the necessary machinery to prepare the fresh food. It was not unusual for the management team to be sweeping the floors and to not be out of the building until eight o'clock in the evening. My back began to complain at the physical exertion of carrying forty-pound blocks of cheese and using other heavy machinery. As a gentle aside, I was put off cream for life (no bad thing!) by putting out all the fresh cream cakes on the counters before the department store opened for business.

I was still going out with my boyfriend, who was not a Christian, and there were increased tensions within our relationship as he wanted to become more physically intimate. I constantly ran away from the prospect and withdrew into myself. I appreciated the fact that no one from church commented on the relationship with my boyfriend or tried to coerce me into finishing with him. I suspect if they had, my belligerent, stubborn streak would have kicked in and I would have done the very opposite! As it was, I came to the natural conclusion over time that I had to end our relationship, as it was not proving compatible with growing and developing my Christian faith.

My faith was deepened in several ways; the first was through reading Christian books. However, that wasn't a straightforward process as Watford did not possess a Christian bookshop, and this was in the days prior to online shopping! A general bookshop did stock a couple of shelves with books on faith, which were just about adequate. Secondly, I started to attend the yearly Spring Harvest event which inspired me to seek changes to my life. Spring Harvest began in 1979 in Prestatyn and was then held in the Butlins' holidays camps at Minehead and Skegness. People from all ages still attend the week's teaching and worship programmes, either with members from their own church or individually. If you have never encountered Spring Harvest, it is well worth looking at its website.[2]

Five years of being a food manager with British Home Stores finally took their toll on my back, which was

---

[2] www.springharvest.org (accessed 18th June 2020).

complaining bitterly! I decided it was time to leave and in 1982 embarked on a year's secretarial course at the local college, which gave my body time to recover. I had had no intention of taking this course and only did so on the advice of the Baptist minister who led the church I attended. His guidance was to be proved prophetically[3] correct, as many years later I would need to use those valuable administrative skills. I enjoyed the course and seemed to have a natural talent in learning shorthand. I did create some mischief at times, as it got rather boring learning all the shorthand techniques!

During the year I spent at college I decided to write to Scripture Union to pose the question about when it was going to open a Christian bookshop in Watford. My letter arrived on the desk of the regional bookshops' manager the very same day he had a meeting with other senior colleagues to discuss where Scripture Union bookshops should expand to next! As I got to know the regional manager, he teased me about the flowery biblical paper I had used when writing to him! Our friendship continues to this day and he is a special man, powerfully used by God in many diverse ministries.

With Scripture Union's encouragement, I started a small group with like-minded people to pray for a Christian bookshop to be opened in Watford. As a young Christian I had no fears in praying for the impossible. It was the first time in Scripture Union's history that it took on board opening a brand-new bookshop. Up until then,

---

[3] Prophecy involves stating something that is going to happen in the future (see Deuteronomy 18:18), but can also be seen as a 'forth-telling' from the heart of God.

when approached by other organisations, it had always taken over established bookshops.

The venture was almost hijacked when we discovered that the road where the shop Scripture Union hoped to lease was located was used by football supporters on Saturdays. Many other shops on the same road would close early on Saturdays, as they feared damage to their properties. To its credit, Scripture Union continued to believe this was of God and went ahead with opening the bookshop. Praying for the bookshop was one of the most inspiring activities I had been involved in.

During this process I didn't make any assumptions that I would be part of running the bookshop. I completed my college course and succeeded in gaining a temporary job working for a department store in Watford as a secretary. In 1984 I sensed God guiding me to join Scripture Union. I trained at its London bookshop for a few months and then joined the bookshop in Watford as an assistant.

I saw first-hand how God provided for the shop in those early days, and it was breathtaking at times. There were occasions when we felt under 'attack' as the electricity would suddenly go off, and one day the lock to the front door had had superglue put in it. We proved a few people wrong by achieving our targeted financial budgets much earlier than expected. We also saw people's lives being changed as they regularly came into the bookshop and chatted to the staff.

I enjoyed being part of a team working at the bookstalls at various annual large Christian festivals all over the country. One year I was helping at an event in Cornwall and decided it would be fun to camp, as it was summertime. Halfway through the week I had to telephone home and ask my housemate to send me some extra socks and other warm clothing, as it was constantly raining. Eventually I had to abandon my tent and spent the last few days sharing a caravan with a couple who were also helping on the bookstall. It was still fun!

During my time at the Baptist church, I became close to a family who lived just around the corner from me. I got to know each of the two children from a very young age. It was the only time in my life that I got broody, when child number two was born. I experienced a joy and a natural healing through spending time with the children.

The family once threw a surprise birthday party for me and I had to seek refuge in their kitchen as I couldn't handle the attention. Their additional gift of baking me a birthday cake blew me away as I had never received one previously. They still hold a precious place in my heart and God has used them all to initiate different layers of healing.

I spent five wonderful years working at the bookshop, despite making little personal headway in tackling the inner demons from my childhood. I had taken over managing the shop when the previous manager left for another role. I desperately wanted my relationship with God to change from an intellectual one to a much more heart-centred rapport. Unfortunately, I had no idea how to let that happen.

In my late twenties, a 'freak accident' occurred while I was playing football in the local park with my twin sister's children who had come to spend a few days with me. This became the catalyst that God used to begin to answer my prayers. As I was kicking the football, I felt something 'go' in my right leg and within a week I was struggling to walk and was in extreme pain.

The next five years of my life revolved around being flat on my back, struggling with chronic pain and starting on a long, tortuous process of inner healing. There were times during those years where I feared I had been put on the scrapheap as I couldn't see an end to the physical pain. I was sharing a house with two other young ladies who had literally only moved in a few weeks before my accident. They were incredibly supportive and caring, no matter what my mood was like on any given day.

4
INPUT Pain Management Unit

During 1990 I reluctantly resigned my position as the bookshop manager with Scripture Union, even though the company was averse to accepting my decision. I didn't feel it was right to keep leaving my job open without any idea how long I would be struggling with physical pain that prevented me from working. I was very grateful to God for the way He provided for me on every level during this time. My income was obviously greatly reduced, yet whenever I needed to pay a bill, the money was always provided through the kindness of friends.

My GP warned me that it was unlikely that anything medically could be done to resolve the pain. When I felt I had come to a place of accepting there was no medical cure, she would be ready and willing to refer me to an inpatient pain management unit (INPUT). In the meantime, she referred me to the Royal National Orthopaedic Hospital in Stanmore, Middlesex, which carried out a procedure to release the tension in one of my nerves at the top of my groin. There was some initial improvement, which raised my hopes, but unfortunately the pain returned and persisted as before. The hospital felt there was nothing more they could do, and discharged me.

Because I had been seen by one of the best hospitals in the country, I didn't feel there was any need to seek a second opinion. At that point I asked my GP to refer me to the specialised pain management unit in London that she had mentioned a while back, who would teach me how to manage my pain.

By that stage, my pain had become chronic, which is very different from acute pain. There is often some confusion around acute and chronic pain, and between pain management centres and pain management units. Acute pain is usually short term, rarely lasting longer than six months. Chronic pain is ongoing and can continue even after the injury that caused it has healed or gone away. Acute pain, if it needs to be treated at a hospital, can be dealt with at a pain management centre where nerve blocks, medication and/or a TENS[4] machine are used to resolve the problem. Chronic pain sufferers need to be referred to pain management programmes where no medical intervention is carried out.

When I was referred to INPUT it was still in its embryonic stages and they were offering people the opportunity to take part in a randomised research project they were undertaking. While being assessed, I agreed to take part in the research, which meant if I was selected, my physical, emotional and psychological measurement scores collated over a year would become part of their research.

I attended a four-week inpatient course at the INPUT unit, which at that time was based in Brixton, London, with five other people. It was interesting that some people

---

[4] Transcutaneous Electric Nerve Stimulation.

would not travel to the unit in Brixton because they were too fearful of the area's reputation! I had no qualms about attending; my priority was to find a way to manage my pain in order to function again.

It was the first time I encountered a multidisciplinary team working together to bring a package of care to help people manage all aspects of their chronic pain. I learned many holistic life-changing techniques to help me take control of the physical pain, which by this time was affecting every area of my life. When pain becomes chronic, it is no longer purely a physical problem. It determined what I could or couldn't do on any given day, it affected my sleep patterns, and mood swings were inevitable with depression often not far away.

On a so-called 'good day' I would overdo activities which then resulted in increased pain and the need to rest more. This became a regular yo-yo pattern. As mentioned before, I feared being on the scrapheap in terms of whether I would ever regain employment. Because nothing showed up on my medical X-rays, there was always a sense of some people not believing I was in pain and they were less than supportive. It was also rather demoralising to attempt to go for a walk and to be overtaken by elderly folk!

The multidisciplinary team who ran the pain management programmes consisted of a consultant anaesthetist, a clinical psychologist, a physiotherapist, a nurse and an occupational therapist. Between them they covered all aspects of pain management.

The consultant anaesthetist educated us on what goes on in the body when chronic pain impacts, and how the spinal gate at the base of the spine was constantly sending pain messages to the brain owing to damaged nerves. One of the most helpful pieces of information we were given is that you cannot invent pain. It may not be seen on X-rays or other tests, but it is genuine.

The psychologist encouraged us to look at what messages we were giving ourselves in relation to our pain: were we constantly criticising ourselves for not mastering the pain? And how did we deal with low mood and depressive thoughts? We looked at how we communicated our needs to those closest to us.

The physiotherapist taught everyone specific exercises relating to their individual pain as well as other strengthening keep-fit movements, but at a paced level. In the first few days we were asked to see how many of the allotted exercises we could manage. That figure was then halved as a baseline to avoid overdoing and to encourage the pacing approach. The exercises were gently increased as the weeks went on but always with the aim of discouraging any flare-up of pain.

The nurse helped people to look at their sleep patterns and encouraged us not to clock-watch; if we couldn't sleep, it was better to get up than to keep tossing and turning in bed. We were asked to get up at the same time each day, irrespective of how much sleep we had had. Bearing in mind I attended my course in the summer months with blistering heatwaves and the added distraction of being under a flight path to Heathrow Airport, sleep was in short supply!

We were taught meditation and reflective exercises by the nurse to distract us when the pain increased. A number of people who attended the programme were on very strong pain medication, antidepressants and sleeping tablets. Thankfully, my GP had discouraged me from taking any of these and I was very grateful to her. The nurse encouraged people to look at their medication and to gradually reduce some of their tablets in a controlled manner, as so often the body simply gets used to a painkiller and then demands more and more.

The occupational therapist worked with each of the participants to discover what our tolerances were concerning the pain we suffered when doing any basic movement. We were issued with a kitchen timer and asked to work out what our tolerances were concerning how far we could walk, or how long we could stand and sit, before we experienced pain. Once the pain hit, we were advised that we had already overdone things. Once we had worked out our tolerances to each of those basic movements, they were also halved and that became our baseline, in the same way as the exercise regime.

The aim was to use our personal timings while undertaking activities; for instance, when washing up, if my baseline for standing was five minutes, my timer would then go off and I would sit on a stool to continue the activity for my sitting tolerance of three minutes. I would repeat this process for as long as it took to finish the household task. By changing our physical position frequently, we were able to break up the faulty messages that were being transmitted to our brain through the spinal gate. Pacing was the key message.

Amazingly, it worked! We gently increased those times until we felt comfortable with balancing our changing positions without causing a flare-up of pain. We were encouraged to put in several rest periods during the day with the aim of avoiding the yo-yo pattern many of us had experienced.

We were discouraged from talking about our pain so that it stopped being the centre of our attention. The objective was to place it on the back burner of our lives, but to always respect it and ensure we managed our pain as well as possible. We were warned that we would still have flare-ups, however. During those occasions we were taught to reduce our tolerance timing levels concerning our movements and our exercises and then to build them back up slowly once the flare-up had calmed down.

Changing our physical movements was encouraged in all our activities – going for a walk, sitting at a computer, going out for a meal, etc. It took confidence and courage to keep to our pain tolerances – for instance, going to a restaurant where others may have wondered what on earth we were doing. In reality, few people noticed whether we were sitting, kneeling, standing up or going walkabout. The most important factor to hold on to was: who would be the one suffering from increased pain if we overdid things?

The challenge of changing positions frequently was really tested in the last week of our four-week programme, when the unit had been invited to take part in a television interview on managing chronic pain. Staff and pain sufferers (including myself) joined in, and I remember taking some deep breaths while needing to constantly change my position during the live recording of the interviews.

People travelled from all over the country to attend the pain management programmes. Accommodation was provided during the four weeks and we were encouraged to go home at least once, if not twice, over the weekends. The aim was to gain confidence in putting into practice in our home environments all we were being taught, so that if we made mistakes, we could quickly regain momentum while still on the programme.

At the beginning of our four-week course we had undertaken a series of physical exercises, and we took them again at the end to see what changes we had made. Some people found they were doing less, as they had stopped trying to beat the pain and were now working on a managed regime of exercise. We also filled in a series of psychological questionnaires to see how our mood and attitudes had or hadn't changed through the programme. These were repeated at one, six and twelve months after we had finished the course.

At the beginning of the programme my tolerances were extremely low; I could only do each of the specific movements for thirty seconds before pain hit. But I quickly gained confidence in seeing how all the techniques were being holistically taught, with the ultimate goal of managing my pain. My body struggled to increase the timings of changing my position, and, after frequent flare-ups over the following months, I was encouraged to stay with five minutes each of sitting, standing and walking. That may have sounded very limiting and frustrating to many people, but I was so pleased at being able to achieve tasks, it frankly didn't matter that it took much longer to complete jobs. The course enabled me to get back on my feet, albeit in a slow and paced manner, and I was delighted.

After completing the four-week programme I stayed on as a volunteer and used the opportunity to rebuild my physical stamina, slowly increasing my working hours as I grew stronger. The unit moved from Brixton to temporary accommodation and came under the umbrella of St Thomas' Hospital, London, though it was still a registered charity. In due course I was offered a part-time job at the unit, which then grew into a full-time position as administrator. Those secretarial skills I had learned came to the forefront! The unit was eventually offered permanent accommodation in a bespoke building where the patients' living quarters and the teaching rooms were all under one roof. I was fortunate to have my office facing the Houses of Commons.

There was something incredibly special about the INPUT unit. I never lost the sense of awe when seeing many people attend a pain management programme using crutches or a wheelchair or limping badly at the beginning, then four weeks later leaving the unit without the need of those aids and walking upright. It didn't matter how old you were or how long you had been suffering with chronic pain. Those factors were not the priorities; the most important factor was whether people had reached that crossroads in their lives in recognising that there was no medical cure for their pain? Only when people had reached that point in acknowledging that their pain was chronic and they were willing to look at how to manage it themselves could the pain management techniques begin to take effect.

The unit became a renowned centre of excellence in helping people to manage chronic pain not only in this country but overseas as well. Many of the staff became prominent speakers at conferences and were involved in major research into chronic pain. When I attended my

47

course, there were only two pain management inpatient units in the country. Thankfully, that figure has risen over the years and pain management units can now be accessed more readily nationwide. The unit at St Thomas' was able to expand its programmes to an outpatient one and to a two-week course to help more people struggling with chronic pain.

As I look back on that time, I recognise how God began to sow the seeds of very different work He had lined up for me (not that I was aware of that then). I also knew how much I valued working in a multidisciplinary team and wanted to continue in that environment.

One of the extra skills I learned during my time at INPUT was the value of a therapeutic environment. We were incredibly fortunate to have one of the top London architects working with the unit for a while. He designed a conservatory which held an incredible array of plants for people to enjoy and look after. He also constructed some astonishing innovative furniture and equipment for each of the teaching rooms. He then went on to engage in a research project with the senior clinical psychologist on the benefits of a therapeutic environment. Wherever possible I have tried to replicate that idea in my other working roles. I personally know I feel more comfortable in a room that isn't cluttered, is decorated well and that has good natural light. I once turned down a job solely on the basis that the office I would be based in was pokey and had no windows!

5
Addressing My Emotional Frailties

God used the difficult years of my struggling with physical pain from the leg injury I had sustained to begin some major 'internal surgery'. As I looked back on that incident in the park with my sister's children, I recognised it had triggered a kind of emotional breakdown. My GP, who was incredibly astute and wise, gently encouraged me to seek some professional counselling.

I had started to trust my GP a little and had shared minute amounts of information about my childhood with her during previous appointments. She sensed my body had 'gone on strike' as my mental capacity and sheer willpower to keep carrying the hidden burdens of my childhood were finally exhausted. For as long as I needed, she committed herself to seeing me every month to keep a check on my mental well-being. I valued her calm manner and her overall support. I was amazed several years later when she wrote a lovely card to me, wishing me well, as I had shared with her about a new venture I was hoping to pursue.

My GP also understood my dilemma, on one of my visits to her, when I talked about my brother becoming a father to his own children. I had not been able to prevent his abuse to me, but I was adamant I would not be found guilty of remaining silent if there was any danger to his offspring. The problem was that I lived too far away to be able to observe how he interacted with his children. She was willing to make an official investigation, if at any stage it was deemed necessary, which was a huge relief to me.

The experience of being laid aside was fundamental in finally halting my continual fleeing from the humungous damage that had been inflicted on me mentally, emotionally, spiritually and physically during my childhood. My GP warned me the counselling would be a long, painful process and would take up to eight years. She turned out to be totally correct in the length of time I needed to mentally work through the abuse I had endured. However, the first stage of finding the right counsellor proved to be less than easy.

Initially, I was referred to the NHS, and the first person I saw called my brother a psychopath, which I didn't take kindly to. If anyone had the right to call him that it was me! I declined the offer to receive support from her. The next person I was referred to was based at a centre on the outskirts of London and was less than welcoming, as he remained silent throughout most of the assessment. As I also remained silent (from a perverse and stubborn attitude), it wasn't exactly a fruitful exercise!

Both of those disappointing encounters took up a considerable amount of time as I endured the inevitable waiting lists for each of the initial assessments. My GP then encouraged me to take matters into my own hands. I had heard quite a lot about an organisation called Childline through watching a Sunday evening programme, *That's Life*, presented by Esther Rantzen.

Childline was established in 1986 by Esther Rantzen in response to a plea from children who were needing support on many issues. Fifty thousand children phoned Childline on its first night.[5]

So I took a deep breath and decided to contact them for some advice. They were incredibly helpful and pointed me in the right direction to an excellent organisation based in London, the Westminster Counselling Foundation. I took another deep breath and telephoned them to request an appointment.

Once I had completed my pain management programme, I attended my initial assessment at the Counselling Foundation, which thankfully went well. After a few months' wait, I was assigned to see a counsellor at the centre on one of the days I volunteered at the pain management unit. Even though I knew this counsellor was the right person to work with, it was to take many years before I started to properly trust her.

I must admit I was miffed at having to spend so much money over the years on counselling, even though I fully appreciated and was grateful for the reduced rate I was generally asked to pay. It still seemed wholly unfair that I was having to pay in monetary terms and to invest so much time and energy to undo the damage from the abuse others had inflicted upon me. However, I needed to put that aside as it was important to hold on to the bigger and healthier picture concerning the reasons why I had embarked on counselling.

The awful events that happened to me and to many others cannot be changed in the very fact that they

---

[5] www.childline.org.uk (accessed 6th July 2020).

occurred. But God offers each one of us a new way forward. We all have choices about whether we spend the rest of our lives in that very understandable 'damaged place' within us, or whether we start to believe in the God of compassion who longs to bring renewal. I was desperate to be freed from the inner baggage from my childhood, and slowly began to believe God was able to bring my desire to fruition.

I played an incredibly good game of keeping my counsellor at arm's length, which I knew she was aware of. In return, she stayed patient and committed to me. I disliked intensely having to go to counselling and told very few people for fear of being mocked or judged.

As the counselling sessions progressed, I began to identify, with my therapist, many patterns of faulty thinking, all of which were totally understandable. I started to see how much fear covered up very strong emotions and how hard I worked at not letting go. There were many faulty messages reigning in my head and we worked on changing my internal 'record tape' and on how to stop listening to the lies of my parents.

I had always feared crying as I believed no one would be there for me, thereby increasing the level of despair and abandonment within me. It felt easier to pretend that what had gone on during my childhood hadn't hurt, that I had no needs, as the emotional and psychological pain would be too great if I were to face the truth. I recognised that the understandable layers of self-sufficiency, pride and not needing anyone, which I had built around me, were not helpful. I acknowledged the feelings of being emotionally frozen inside and how anger was a totally unacceptable sentiment to me.

I was incredibly matter-of-fact when describing to my counsellor the layers of abuse that had been inflicted on me. I battled with disclosing the much deeper feelings of shame, revulsion, guilt, a sense of collusion and the bartering for survival. The whole process felt like I was constantly walking through a minefield.

One of the main patterns I had to repeatedly work on was wanting to do a 'head-on collision' in forcing change, especially in wanting to weep. I had come to the place of desperately wanting to press the cry switch, but of course it wouldn't happen at my command! I got desperately tired of being patient, the weekly discipline of attending counselling and the intensity of all that I needed to work through. I fought to stay in control and to stay rational. I got annoyed with my counsellor when she didn't and wouldn't collude with me!

There were so many periods of feeling utterly exhausted from working through all the years of abuse. Unravelling the burdens I had carried as a child through to adulthood was massive. Admitting to the emotionally and physically impoverished way my parents had treated me was deeply painful. I knew many of the vows I had made as a child held me back, and so I constantly faced the challenge of whether I was prepared to let them go; for example, I had vowed never to let anyone close enough to 'mother' me, or, in fact, to trust any adult.

There were occasions when I wondered if I would ever come out the other side of all I had to process in the therapy sessions. It often felt like a relentless grind. I went through periods of disturbed sleep, distressing nightmares, intrusive thoughts and many, many flashbacks. Some weeks were torrid; I experienced constant fears of being overwhelmed. I felt drained, stressed and stretched. I had a strong image of me as a child, marooned, untouchable and unable to reach out in any shape or form. I reached a place of utter despair, a sense of being at the bottom of a pit. I sensed waves of depression around me, and daily living felt like I was eating sawdust.

My counsellor was very aware of all these complexities and was careful with the pace of our work together. When I tried to rush things, she slowed them down. She knew how important the issue of control was for me, and always made sure to inform me when our sessions were reaching the end of an hour, so there was no abrupt ending. She also understood my fears around silence and helped me to manage the start of our sessions, where therapists usually wait for their clients to say how they want to use their hour together.

Five years later, my counsellor moved her practice to her home in Loughton, Essex, which meant an even longer commuting journey. I initially saw her at a doctor's surgery before eventually seeing her at her home address. Each change triggered fresh anxieties as I adjusted to the new environment. I had been an expert at blanking out so many memories and the emotions that went alongside them. This was specifically highlighted when I started seeing my therapist at her house. There was a single bed on the left of the room we used, but I had totally ignored it. The time came when my counsellor suggested I lay down on it and my reply was, 'I would rather throw it out of the window!'

It took a while before I felt able to change my sitting position to a horizontal one. As I did so, fresh emotions were evoked which needed to be looked at, and in the ongoing process began to be freed up. It became another healthy step forward in trusting my counsellor. The times I became vulnerable with her were key and crucial to my growth. I came to a point of being able to verbalise that I needed her, and allowed her into some of the most traumatic memories. That signified incredible progress, given how much had needed untangling within me in terms of trusting an adult.

We discussed increasing our sessions to twice a week, which I initially baulked at. However, I trusted my therapist enough by then to realise this would prove beneficial, and went ahead. As I did so, I finally stopped playing the games of holding her at arm's length and began to trust her in a much deeper way. Interestingly, it speeded up the therapeutic process, and six months or so later we started to look at my sessions drawing to a close.

6

Improving My Spiritual Journey

During the period I had spent flat on my back from my leg injury, I had stopped attending church. I had tried to keep attending by lying down on some chairs at the back but I felt too awkward and felt as if I was 'on show'. I hadn't given up on my faith in God, but I was fed up of constantly facing the questions around why I hadn't been healed as people had prayed. I had continued to go to a house group, which very good friends of mine ran. They were equally frustrated by people giving me a hard time about why God hadn't healed my leg.

Leading up to one particular house-group meeting, my friends pleaded with me not to engage with the constant questioning, so I promised them I would stay silent, which I did. However, they got so annoyed by what people were asking me that they stepped in to protect and defend me. The three of us realised there was no way forward, and I gave up attending the group. I doggedly refused to go back to church for about ten years.

Right from the start of embarking on the counselling process, I asked God to be at the centre of all that it would involve. I clearly knew at some point He would provide a spiritual element of healing, but I also recognised that for the first few years of therapy it was vital to work through the immense mental damage that had been done to my psyche. Nevertheless, I didn't want my relationship with God to be impacted in any negative way.

I was grateful to God for the ability He gave me to know within myself when I had come through a certain stage in processing the very difficult emotions and memories. I clearly sensed when I was still not quite 'there' with a specific issue. I equally knew how important it was to be gentle, accepting and tolerant with myself. I realised, albeit grudgingly, that there were no short cuts. God was very aware how much I could take at any one time. That meant that sometimes I would need to revisit some of those difficult emotions at a later phase in life.

As I spent time with God at the start of the counselling, I sensed Him ask me what changes I wanted to see happen within me. At that point, I knew I needed to let go of those areas of my inner being dominated by the conflicts between striving, being passive, stubbornness and fighting. I wanted to experience more of a love relationship with God, rather than the disciplined 'head' relationship that was predominantly centre stage.

During the long journeys to see my counsellor after a day's work in London, and then the even longer journeys home via public transport, I began to experience for the first time a different relationship with Jesus. Beforehand, I would ask Him for the necessary wisdom, energy and insight into how to use the session. I would then ask Jesus to carry me as I came away an hour later utterly exhausted, knowing home was at least an hour and a half away.

Of course, there were times I became frustrated because the counselling sessions seemed to dominate my life, and the process was gruelling. When I questioned the need to carry on, I came back to the reasons why I had embarked on it in the first place and held on to how much I wanted to see lasting change within me. There were certainly occasions I feared for my mental well-being, but God remained faithful and continually sustained me.

Throughout the counselling, God would promise me many things and invited me to be as honest with Him as I could. I recognised how much I needed God's strength and courage to emotionally own the pain from my childhood. I sensed Him say to me early in the tortuous process that He would melt my 'heart of stone'[6] and that I would get to the position of being able to begin to relax in His love. There was often a sense of His tenderness and gentleness towards me. I was able to say how much I feared intimacy with Him. His promises echoed throughout my tired brain and body and I knew, despite all the turmoil, that He was at the centre of it all. He would not let me down; He would not let the circumstances overwhelm me. God firmly assured me that He would not be like my parents. He would never abandon me. He fully understood what my parents had failed to give me as I grew up. God was promising to be a father and mother to me, but at a pace I could cope with.

The gift of love

Unlike the complexities of human love, God's love, thankfully, has a very different depth and security. His love is consistent, faithful, utterly undeserved, unconditional, always compassionate and isn't swayed by

---

[6] See Ezekiel 36:26.

events or behaviours. God isn't subject to bad moods, hormonal sways or any of the daily battles we may struggle with in our human relationships. There is something so incredibly comforting and hopeful in holding on to these solid facts of God's steadfast nature.

However, if we haven't experienced human love well, or not at all, as a baby, as a toddler, as a child, as a teenager and as an adult, how on earth can we believe we are loved unconditionally by God? One very large obstacle to believing we are loved intimately by God is that we, of course, look at this painful predicament with human eyes. If we have had no healthy role models to learn from, it's totally understandable that we may feel it is humanly impossible to believe that Father God, who we cannot see, loves us.

What is so astonishing is that God doesn't and never will give up on His children. He waits to be invited; He sows seeds of hope and desire within our hearts and minds as He knows our deepest longings are to have a love relationship with Him. We can take baby, tentative steps in learning to accept and trust that God loves us individually. The invitation to His banquet hall is eternal; there are no opening or closing hours!

As with many of the gifts I am sharing about throughout this book, so much has been written over the centuries about God's love. Personally, I think these verses from Ephesians sum up the amazing and precious gift that God offers each and every one of His children as we seek to know Him more:

> I pray that out of his glorious riches he may strengthen you with power through his Spirit in

your inner being, so that Christ may dwell in your hearts through faith. And I pray that you, being rooted and established in love, may have power, together with all the Lord's holy people, to grasp how wide and long and high and deep is the love of Christ, and to know this love that surpasses knowledge – that you may be filled to the measure of all the fullness of God.
(Ephesians 3:16-19)

God's love is all-encompassing. Meditating on and savouring all that these verses convey to us can be utterly enriching.

When Jesus was on one of His walkabouts, healing many people who came to Him, He explained to His disciples that they only needed to have 'faith as small as a mustard seed' and they could 'say to this mountain, "Move from here to there," and it will move.' I prefer *The Message* translation of this verse, as I can't really picture what a mustard seed looks like. *The Message* quotes Jesus as saying:

The simple truth is that if you had a mere kernel of faith, a poppy seed, say, you would tell this mountain, 'Move!' and it would move. There is nothing you wouldn't be able to tackle.
(Matthew 17:20-21, *The Message*)

I can grasp the poppy seed image better than that of a mustard seed! As a keen gardener I have had poppies galore growing in my garden, and always take delight in opening the dried seed pods after they have finished flowering. As I scatter the minute seeds from the pods onto fresh soil, I know they will produce new beautiful displays of colourful poppies next year. So if we can begin to believe and experience God's love at a 'poppy seed level', that hopefully feels more obtainable in our hearts and minds. There is something extraordinarily generous and personal in God showing how much He loves each of His children by using that analogy of one poppy seed, which we are told can move mountains!

I believe that to be true, as I have experienced God take my minute poppy seed of faith concerning His depth of love for me. I have seen my poppy seed spread, grow and produce so much vibrancy, colour and life within me. We can deepen this incredible truth further by reading other biblical passages alluding to God seeing His children as being very treasured.[7]

Like all human relationships, there will, of course, be times in our lives when love is tested, and it is no different concerning our rapport with God. When we go through crises, we may, understandably, question or doubt that we are still precious and loved. Love isn't simply a warm, fuzzy feeling. If it was, it wouldn't endure the difficulties many people go through during their lifetimes. We would also be in danger of becoming 'spoilt'. It is during those times of crisis that we need to stay rooted in the rock-solid promises available to us by reading God's Word, by praying to stay close to Him, and by asking others for support.

People have shared with me that when they are going through difficult times, they discover who their real friends are – individuals who have been willing to stay

---

[7] See, for example, Deuteronomy 7:6; 1 John 3:1.

close to them. They have often been surprised at those who have run away and those who have remained solid. Thankfully, God is faithful, and we can be reassured that He will never, ever run away from us!

As I explained earlier, I began the counselling process cringing at the word 'intimacy' and would quickly withdraw and put my internal barriers up at the prospect of being loved, as it felt too painful, too threatening and far too intrusive. Today, I am, thankfully, in an entirely different place spiritually and emotionally. I am no longer fearful of God's love for me and I can enjoy that inner, intimate relationship that is available to each of God's children.

Some people may be familiar with the chapter in 1 Corinthians[8] that is often shared during a wedding service. It illustrates the plethora of attributes of God's love. A while back, I spent some time paraphrasing what the chapter personally meant to me in describing how I experience God's love: personal, mind-blowing, kind, protective, honourable, hopeful, enduring, monumental, eternal, outrageous, sacrificial, healing, respectful, sincere, transforming, forgiving, faithful, gracious, generous, consistent, trustworthy, patient, delightful, unconditional, intimate, steadfast, persevering, perfect, awesome, compassionate and truthful.

Spending time thinking about how God loves each of us unconditionally and how He accepts us just as we are is an incredibly healthy exercise. I have been so awestruck at the depth of His love for me and His welcoming invitation to spend time with Him at His banquet hall. We

---

[8] 1 Corinthians 13.

are all invited to drink deeply and abide in His presence, to rest in a place of intimacy and safety, lost in the awe and wonder of the sheer and utter privilege of being His daughter or His son, His prince or His princess, being able to let go of all the other 'stuff' that can drag us down, and simply drink in His love.

There are so many exquisite references throughout the Bible where God offers to be our 'rock', our 'fortress',[9] our 'hiding-place',[10] and how He invites us to shelter 'in the shadow of [His] wings'.[11] Some verses from Psalm 91 illustrate that:

> Whoever dwells in the shelter of the Most High
> will rest in the shadow of the Almighty.
> I will say of the LORD, 'He is my refuge and my fortress,
> my God, in whom I trust.'
> Surely he will save you
> from the fowler's snare
> and from the deadly pestilence.
> He will cover you with his feathers,
> and under his wings you will find refuge;
> his faithfulness will be your shield and rampart.
> (Psalm 91:1-4)

The Father's love negates all fear; it is fully embracing and turns negativity upside down. God will always be my rock if I allow Him to be; He offers to hold my hand, to walk alongside me. I am now in a place where I know I love

---

[9] Psalm 18:2; 2 Samuel 22:2.
[10] Psalm 32:7.
[11] Psalm 17:8.

Him because He welcomes me with unconditional, non-judgemental love. He is altogether gentle, generous, spontaneous and outrageously uncondemning. He is all I need and is there constantly with an embrace, a hand, an attentive heart and a listening ear.

That I am able to write these powerful, all-encompassing truths is nothing short of a miracle when I consider my childhood. There were occasions when God generously gave me 'pictures'[12] to help as I worked through certain issues during the counselling process. He gave me an initial image of an iron box around the deepest emotions of my being. Another illustration was of being in a room that was pitch black, and I was aware of feelings of terror, being so alone and abandoned. As I spent time with this image, God's gentle light came into the room of darkness and He gently reminded me He was there.

Thankfully, there were breaks in the intensity of the therapy and I valued the time to re-energise. I sensed the inner shackles were being loosened. It was useful to keep a journal throughout those years as this helped me to hold on to all the changes that were happening. The journals were also a helpful reminder when things got tougher. I held on to one specific prayer I had penned in one journal:

> I want to dedicate all parts of myself to You, and to ask You, Jesus, to be in the middle of each stage I go through. In all of my fears, scars, hurts and memories of the abuse, I ask for Your love. In my vulnerabilities, may I constantly hold Your hand

---

[12] God sometimes gives His people 'pictures' or images to illustrate or reveal something to them.

and seek Your arms of love, strength, courage and hope.

I can safely say God has honoured that prayer with His incredible gift of love.

7
Changes Ahead

When I celebrated my fortieth birthday, I decided I wanted to learn to drive. My father had taught my other siblings to drive while they were young but, not surprisingly, hadn't given me the same opportunity.

I had no idea how fraught and scary this exercise would prove to be. It was like every fear in the book emerged in me! There is a well-known fact that the older you are when you start to learn to drive, the harder it is, and I certainly discovered how true that was. I realised I had a problem with coordination when I attempted to manoeuvre the steering wheel full circle. I had to practise at home rotating a dinner plate to encourage my brain to get the message!

I managed to pass my driving test at the second attempt. The first test didn't bode well when the person who was examining me got into the passenger seat and proceeded to yawn. When I am nervous, I can come out with inappropriate remarks, and I heard myself say, 'Am I boring you?' It was not a great start!

It was through my driving instructor, who was a Christian, that I eventually agreed to go back to church. He would spend at least half of the driving lessons nagging me to return to church! In the end I decided to give it a go, but vowed to God the only way I would do so would be with the 'masks off', and I determined that I would seek a different relationship with Him.

I started to attend an Anglican church in the evenings, where a more reflective style of service was held. It was there that God initiated another layer of healing within me, which I had so yearned for. I also began to regularly meet up with a friend who attended the same church, and it was clear to see that she was God's channel as we spent time talking and praying together. It was a special, fruitful season as I began to grow in a way I had long thought was impossible.

Life continued in that vein for quite some time, with the combination of the ongoing counselling and the gradual spiritual growth through spending time praying with my friend. Change was around the corner, though, with the news that my father had been given a terminal diagnosis of pancreatic cancer. He was given eighteen months to live, at the most. Amazingly, I had maintained an ongoing relationship with my parents, though I fully recognised it was purely from a 'dutiful daughter' angle.

I recall the day I walked to the local shops with my mother not long after my father had been given his terminal diagnosis. An inner dialogue was going on in my mind as I recognised afresh how much I hated both my parents. Outwardly, no one would have known how those feelings provoked an ongoing inward conflict. I knew as a Christian it was spiritually incorrect to harbour feelings of hate. I was familiar with all the teaching around forgiveness and the price that Jesus had paid for me with His death on the cross.

The gift of salvation I had received and accepted at the time I had come to faith meant a huge amount. I also knew God didn't want me using up extra emotional and spiritual energy holding on to the inner conflicting feelings concerning the whole subject of forgiveness. I sensed God was using this internal dialogue to prompt and encourage me to go a stage deeper in the healing process around the area of forgiveness before my father died. As a result, there was a renewed focus to my counselling sessions. It was essential I made the most of the time and the opportunities I had from the onset of my father's diagnosis and not to have any regrets at his death when it happened.

The gift of forgiveness

Whole books have been written on the topic of forgiveness and it is impossible to cover such a significant topic within the context of this chapter. Suffice to say, forgiveness is one of the most awe-inspiring gifts God chooses to offer to His children, not only at the beginning of our relationship with Him, but also whenever we need His cleansing touch in our lives. He never comes to the end of His grace and mercy in absolving His children when we have messed up. Unlike humanity, He thankfully doesn't hold on to our past mistakes or berate us for our frailties.

There are, as with all of God's gifts, different strands of forgiveness readily available for all of us to access at any point. Some of us will have experienced a depth of being pardoned as we have come to faith and accepted Jesus as our Saviour and Friend. Many of us will know, out of a love that is beyond human comprehension, how God has paid for this incredible gift of forgiveness by sacrificing His Son, Jesus, on the cross. One of the most well-known verses in the Bible affirms God's ultimate sacrifice that enables us to receive His forgiveness: 'For God so loved the world that he gave his one and only Son, that whoever believes in him shall not perish but have eternal life' (John 3:16).

God has literally given everything to enable His children to partake in the most awesome, ongoing, lifetime relationship. He is outrageously generous. Within this incredible affinity, God expects His children to talk to Him about the things we may have said or done that have caused offence or pain to others.

We may feel that we have made so many mistakes in our lives that God will not include us in that place of absolution. One of the difficult aspects of forgiveness can be believing that God's pardon is enough and that He has 'wiped the slate clean'. Sometimes we can struggle to exonerate ourselves and seem hell-bent on punishing, criticising and judging our frailties. We fail to hear God say those precious words, 'I forgive you, my child.'

Not only are we good at passing judgement on our own weaknesses, but the world is quick to add its accusations too. There are different encounters in the Gospels where Jesus is rebuked, either by the crowds or by the Pharisees and teachers of the law, for mixing with 'disreputable people'. For example, in Luke's Gospel we read how Jesus had been invited to eat at Simon the Pharisee's house (Luke 7:36-50). While there, He was anointed by a woman who had 'lived a sinful life'. She had brought an 'alabaster jar of perfume' with her and anointed Jesus' feet, weeping as she did so. The other guests at the meal were horrified, and you can imagine the tutting and shaking of heads.

Another way the world places judgement on people is to condemn those suffering with a physical ailment by stating their illness is a consequence of sin. It's fascinating to read the Gospels, and in all the times where Jesus is interacting with the people around Him, He only talks about forgiveness once in the context of healing. We read how Jesus forgave the paralysed man who was lowered through a roof by his friends, as He was teaching (Luke 5:17-20). Jesus does not use the words of forgiveness found in verse 20 in any other act of healing throughout His teaching.

As God has forgiven His children so generously, He expects us to do the same when we have disagreements with people we interact with. He doesn't want us to use up emotional and spiritual energy holding on to grudges. In his letter to the Ephesians, Paul exhorts the people not to retire to bed at the end of a day while still angry, but to put matters right (Ephesians 4:26). Interestingly, Paul makes the distinction of it being OK to be angry, but not to stew over conflict. I think we have all been in that position where something has gone wrong and the incident keeps going around and around in our heads!

What's astounding is that even when Jesus was enduring a torturous death on the cross, He offered forgiveness to one of the two criminals who were also being crucified alongside Him:

> One of the criminals who hung there hurled insults at him: 'Aren't you the Messiah? Save yourself and us!'

But the other criminal rebuked him. 'Don't you fear God,' he said, 'since you are under the same sentence? We are punished justly, for we are getting what our deeds deserve. But this man has done nothing wrong.'

Then he said, 'Jesus, remember me when you come into your kingdom.'

Jesus answered him, 'Truly I tell you, today you will be with me in paradise.'
(Luke 23:39-43)

When we have suffered at the hands of others and have the emotional and physical scars to continually contend with, forgiveness can be incredibly complex. There are no formulae for the process of clemency when dealing, for instance, with abuse, continual criticism or bullying. It is not at all helpful or healthy when others blandly assume all we must do is to verbally pardon the person or persons who have caused such damage.

Thankfully, God is far wiser and more compassionate when coming alongside His children to help them in this difficult and painful place. It is impossible to force the pace at which we can work through the different layers of absolution that may be necessary in these situations. I think it is also imperative that we don't attempt to work this through by ourselves. We need to start at a place of being honest with someone we value and trust. It is then essential to be equally honest and open with God, who already knows our innermost thoughts.

The well-used image of an onion being peeled, layer by layer, is an apt description of the progression of forgiveness that God has taken me through. God has known when I have been ready to face yet another painful round of difficult memories that have necessitated His healing touch. As He has initiated that restoration within me, I have needed to continually work through my responsibility of exonerating my family. It is not enough to superficially absolve my parents and my brother for the appalling depths of abuse they subjected me to and for the many scars I bear as a result. My growth as a child and daughter of my *Abba* Father[13] demands honesty and integrity in the willingness to forgive.

There are times, I know, we may all have said the words, 'Not my will, Lord, but Yours,'[14] when we have struggled to absolve others. We need to reach that place of being able to acknowledge our own helplessness. I have certainly had to come to that position within myself many times. I also recognise and hugely value the awareness of a supernatural element to absolution. Humanly speaking, I know I could not have embarked on the inner depths of pardoning my parents and brother that I have attained without God's continual grace and mercy.

The invitation to enter God's banquet hall, no matter what, is superbly illustrated in Psalm 51 and beautifully sums up God's generosity in His gift of absolution for all His children. Throughout the psalm we read how God's love is unfailing and how He shows great compassion. The psalmist, whom we know is King David, knowing full well he has messed up big time, asks God to wash away his sins and to cleanse him. With a level of intimacy that can take your breath away, he goes on:

---

[13] See, for example, Romans 8:15.
[14] See Luke 22:42.

Create in me a pure heart, O God,
and renew a steadfast spirit within me.
Do not cast me from your presence
or take your Holy Spirit from me.
Restore to me the joy of your salvation
and grant me a willing spirit, to sustain me …
My sacrifice, O God, is a broken spirit;
a broken and contrite heart
you, God, will not despise.
(Psalm 51:10-12,17)

I am not sure I would have reacted as the psalmist did; he knew he had blatantly broken God's commandments in the acts of adultery and murder he had committed. I think I would have hidden away from God, and even if I had been able to accept His words of forgiveness, it would have taken quite a while to believe and receive them. I also sense I would have tried to earn that clemency! The psalmist understood and embraced the gift of absolution God offers.

As I went through the process of preparing for my father's death, I recognised I needed to come away from the daily commute into London and to seek a job locally. It was important to have the freedom to be able to travel to my parents' home as and when necessary. As I prayed for a new job, I realised I wanted to come away from an administrative role, and sought a new challenge. When I saw a research and audit post being advertised at the local hospice in Watford, I immediately knew that was the job God was leading me to.

Leaving the role at the INPUT pain management unit in London was a big wrench. My involvement with them from being a patient to working full-time covered a period of twelve years. They had taught me a great deal in how to manage my chronic pain and had got me back on my feet, and I had thoroughly enjoyed being part of a multidisciplinary team. I still use the skills I was taught there to this day. I also greatly valued many of the friendships I had gained during my time at the unit.

I was offered an interview for the advertised post at the hospice and had an amazing experience while waiting in the reception area beforehand. I had a vivid sense of Jesus picking me up and sitting me on His knee, and of being reassured this was where He wanted me to be. After a rather strange and complicated interview process, I joined the organisation in 2002, but within weeks the job in research and audit became defunct. Instead, I was asked to take on the role of managing all the non-clinical areas of the hospice, which I reluctantly agreed to.

I recognised the hospice was going through quite an extraordinary crisis, though thankfully it did not affect patient care. I was also rather perplexed by people's attitudes towards me in the first few months. I had expected the staff working at the hospice to be warm and welcoming, but I picked up a lot of caution and aloofness towards me. I was eventually informed that they had believed I had been employed to 'spy' on them! Thankfully, they were reassured this was not the case and their attitude towards me changed.

I was somewhat disappointed with this turn of events as I was back to undertaking an administrative role. However, it soon became apparent why God had allowed that to happen. A few months later, I went on a weekend conference with the Anglican church I was attending.

During those few days away, two people independently approached me and asked if I had considered going into the Anglican ministry! I confess I swore at them both as they delivered the message that they believed God had given them for me. I had certainly not seen that coming!

By now, I was mature enough in the Christian faith to know that there was no point fighting God and it was a lot easier to simply wave a white flag and surrender to His plans. That didn't mean I took on board the idea with any degree of joy or excitement. I knew the pitfalls of engaging in full-time Christian work from when I had worked in the bookshop for Scripture Union.

I didn't know the vicar particularly well at the church, as I was still only going in the evenings. However, I knew I needed to talk through with him what had occurred during the church weekend away. I hoped he would agree with me that it wasn't a good idea. When I met up with him, I jokingly offered him £50 if he would say no to the whole concept! Over the next few months, we met up at regular intervals to talk and pray through whether this was of God and to explore the best way forward. I was adamant right from the beginning of the process that if I were to go ahead with this, it would be as a hospice chaplain and not as a parish priest.

Many people who become involved in hospice work find that the whole atmosphere and concept of palliative care tends to get into your blood, and I was no different. I had an amazing line manager at the beginning of my time at the hospice. He challenged me to step away from my desk and to frequently go on walkabout around the building. I had become very proficient at juggling different tasks hidden behind a desk in my previous job, but he turned that concept upside down!

I began to embrace an emotional interaction within the realms of my role, which at first felt scary but was also rewarding. Becoming more emotionally involved in my role while maintaining a high level of professionalism was quite a learning curve. Joining the hospice was one of the most fulfilling and challenging jobs I have undertaken.

I met Sue, who was the physiotherapist at the hospice in 2002, and a very special and unique friendship began and flourished over the coming years. In lots of ways, Sue was the very opposite of me, but we both began to value spending time together. Sue spent many hours listening to me debating whether to go ahead with putting myself forward for the Anglican ministry. She was very familiar with the process, as her husband was also training to become an Anglican priest, and she was training to become a Reader at her local Anglican church. A Reader works alongside an ordained church minister and is licensed to take services, including funerals, and to be involved in other areas of church life depending on their gifting. They are self-funded and their training tends to be on a part-time basis over a number of years.

God initiated different layers of healing for me through my friendship with Sue. She was the first person I began to properly trust, and she taught me how to love without fear. Her gentle and quiet nature encouraged me to share my childhood experiences with her over time, and she understood my anxieties of being rejected by her as I did so. Her commitment and acceptance were evident and helped me considerably in my growth to become the healthy adult I was aiming to be.

In return I encouraged Sue to be more mischievous! We found lots of ways to giggle and laugh together. In the days we worked at the hospice we often had lunch in the park, which was just next door, and there was one bench there that was 'ours'. I was never impressed when someone else dared to sit on it! One lunchtime the heavens decided to open, along with thunder and lightning. After sheltering under a tree (as you do!), hoping for the rain to ease, we had no choice but to walk back to work. The reception staff couldn't believe their eyes as we entered the building soaking wet. We had to find some dressing gowns to put on while our clothes were in the tumble dryer!

Sue was the more confident and experienced driver out of the two of us and therefore relied on my navigating skills when we had time away together. The day she literally took my direction to turn right to find the teashop we were looking for, ended in absolute hysterics. We found ourselves in a field with a bird of prey looking utterly disdainful at the pair of us daring to disturb his peace.

Before I met Sue, she had undergone breast cancer treatment and thankfully had been given the all-clear. She was followed up with annual mammograms, and one of those appointments revealed the disease had unfortunately returned. The day after hearing this difficult news she, of course, came into work! I decided that wasn't happening and, as we had both worked many hours overtime without taking the time back and I possessed enough authority, I signed us both out of the building and we played hooky. We trudged through our favourite woods, trying to get our heads around her disappointing news and eventually came out opposite a pub. On entering the deserted pub, which had only just opened, we asked the bemused barman what we could have with the few pound coins we had between us. Bless him, he provided us with doorstep pieces of toast and pots of tea. We reckoned he was an angel!

Thankfully, through two lots of surgery in the ensuing months and a change in Sue's drug regime, the cancer was once more beaten.

The medical profession proved to be very accurate in the timescale it had given my father, and he visibly began to deteriorate. He agreed to be admitted to his local hospice, as his symptoms were becoming increasingly difficult for my mother to manage on her own, even with the aid of my younger sister. Within a few days of his admission he quickly slipped into a coma, and I received the expected telephone call, while at work, from my younger sister. She asked me to join them at the hospice as she and my mother were needing support.

Over the next few days, I found myself in the extremely bizarre situation of sharing a bed with my mother and both of us sleeping in the same room as my father. Waiting for his inevitable end of life felt difficult at times, and at one stage I telephoned the consultant anaesthetist from the INPUT unit to ask for his advice on what I should expect. He was very helpful and kind in giving me the required information.

On the morning of my father's death, I woke up knowing it would be his last day and prayed for an opportunity to have some space alone with him. That was easier said than done, with five other siblings also wanting time with him. I did manage a few minutes alone with my father and verbally forgave him for the way he had treated me throughout my childhood. I didn't go into any details. I knew he could still hear me even though he was in a coma and, as I spoke to him, I felt his hand respond in mine.

I am extremely grateful to God that I embarked on those layers of forgiveness regarding my father before his death. It meant that I was able to naturally grieve for him without any lingering regrets. It wasn't long after my father's death that I came to the end of my counselling sessions in London, but with the proviso that I could contact my therapist at any stage in the future if I needed to. I was immensely grateful for all we had worked through together and acknowledged I was now in a far better state mentally and emotionally.

The gift of relationship

I also recognised God was preparing me for a different journey which would take me so much deeper into a fulfilling relationship with Him. I have shared previously how my relationship with God in the early years was very much a mind rather than a heart one. When people have suffered childhood abuse and have had no healthy role models in their lives, to experience God as their heavenly Father can, on an emotional level, be excruciatingly difficult. But thankfully God is more than able to bring healing and restoration at levels He knows we are desiring and are ready for. If we take time to study the Song of Songs, we can hopefully grasp the underlying theme of how God wants to woo His children to go deeper and deeper into a life-giving relationship with Him.

I am utterly astounded and deeply humbled by how much my connection with God has changed over these forty years of walking with Him. Two conversations have stayed with me and encouraged me to keep seeking God and not to ever settle for second best. Having an element of perversity and stubbornness has also helped me not to give up!

The first conversation was where a good friend of mine shared how God is a perfect gentleman and will never, ever force His way into our lives; He always waits for permission. He went on to explain how God's love remains consistent, no matter what I do or don't do with my life.

The other conversation involved someone stating that I shouldn't expect to always hear God at an intimate level. If those encounters occurred, they would be few and far between. I disagreed then and I continue to disagree with that well-meant statement. God delights in spending time with His children and He has never been in the business of rationing!

The internationally renowned priest, author and theologian Henri Nouwen wrote more than forty books during his lifetime. One of those books, *The Inner Voice of Love*, was written following a deeply personal crisis. The back cover of this book describes how Nouwen 'suddenly lost his self-esteem, his energy to live and work, his sense of being loved and even his hope in God'.[15] I spent well over a year meditating on the different chapters (each only consisting of one or two pages) of this thought-provoking

---

[15] Henri Nouwen, *The Inner Voice of Love: A Journey Through Anguish to Freedom* (London: Darton, Longman & Todd, 1990).

book and it radically and profoundly helped to change my inner relationship with God. The chapters relate to Nouwen's realisation that 'no human friendship could fulfil the deepest longings of my heart'.[16] It was important for me to pray through the relevant chapters and to stay with them as I allowed God to speak through the words. It is a book I have returned to time and time again, as there are numerous treasures to discover and chew over.

'Who do you say I am?' (Matthew 16:15) was a question Jesus posed at one stage in His affiliation with His disciples. I sensed Jesus asking me the same question during a week I spent on a spiritual retreat, and I replied:

> My Jesus, how I love You for who You are. You are my Risen Lord, my Redeemer, my Saviour. You are holy, awesome and majestic and yet approachable to the point of being able to run into Your arms and be held high by You. You are my Counsellor, my Healer. My inner being dances with You, at other times I shyly hold Your hand. You are always faithful and understanding, offering supernatural healing to those parts of my soul where no human is permitted to enter. You are so utterly gentle, compassionate, fearfully and wonderfully remaking those parts of me which were destroyed as a child. You, Jesus, are my everything, without You I am nothing. I have no meaning, no value, no hope. You are my delight, You set me alight and make me alive. You are my freedom-maker and Creator.

---

[16] Ibid, page xi.

To even be able to write these intimate words demonstrates how far I have travelled in my relationship with Jesus. These words are echoed in an incredible book written by David Benner, who encourages us to:

> Think of Christ as presiding over a banquet at the deep center of our being. His invitation to us is to search out the poor, crippled, blind and lame aspects of our inner self and bring them to his feast of love.[17]

A few sentences further down the page, Benner goes on to illustrate how 'our fearful, angry and wounded parts of self can never be healed unless they are exposed to divine love'.[18] Earlier in the same book, he describes, 'In Jesus, God becomes human and courts us with tenderness and unimaginable kindness.'[19] The gift of a loving relationship is readily available to all of us from God's banquet hall; the challenge is: how much do we want to eat and drink from it?

Alongside my improving rapport with God, I have also experienced the joy of human relationships and have taken huge strides forward in relating to those around me. It has at times been an excruciatingly painful journey, as so often my reaction to being loved was to run away and withdraw. Being self-sufficient, self-contained and very comfortable in my own company had always been the norm for me. I have previously vehemently disagreed

---

[17] David Benner, *Surrender to Love: Discovering the Heart of Christian Spirituality* (Downers Grove, IL: IVP, 2003), p82.
[18] Ibid, p82.
[19] Ibid, p60.

with John Donne's famous quote: 'No man is an island, entire of itself; every man is a piece of the continent, a part of the main.'[20]

You can imagine there have been many tussles with God as He has encouraged and invited me to come away from my self-imposed, safe island! Step by step, I have been able to let go of those vows I made as a child and as a young adult and have learned to trust and to love key people around me.

[20] John Donne, *Devotions: Upon Emergent Occasions, Together with Death's Duel* (Ann Arbor, MI: University of Michigan Press, 1959). The Project Gutenberg's e-book, downloadable, p108. These famous words were not originally written as a poem but were part of one of his sermons.

8

The Call to Priesthood

Coming back to my tentative thoughts around whether I was willing to put myself forward for Anglican ministry, it was time to take a giant leap of faith as my vicar contacted the director of ordinands from the St Albans diocese. Every Anglican diocese has a director of ordinands (DDO) whose role is to work with individuals over quite a period to discern if their calling to the priesthood seems to be a genuine one. All I remember from that first meeting was my relief at driving up the hill to the director's house in one go! I had taken my first driving test in St Albans and failed it because of that dreaded hill as the incline was so steep!

I always looked forward to my meetings with Michael, the DDO, which continued over the next twelve to eighteen months. Bear in mind I had absolutely no idea what it meant to be an Anglican, I knew none of the 'language' and had absolutely no experience of church leadership! I recall one of the very first questions Michael asked me was what I encountered on approaching and entering an Anglican church. Suffice to say, I scrambled around in my brain, trying to think of anything appropriate. Michael's immortal words on hearing my reply were that we had a 'huge mountain to climb'! To his credit, he joined me in that climb, and I know Michael considered me to be 'a breath of fresh air' in my 'ignorance'! Our relationship from the start was a very honest, mutually supportive one.

One of the first exercises I was asked to complete involved going to as many people I could who knew me well, asking them whether they felt I was called to be an Anglican priest. This made me deeply uncomfortable on two levels. Firstly, I didn't like people paying me compliments, which they did as I asked them the question. Secondly, I felt I was in danger of relying on other people's viewpoints. At that stage I hadn't personally heard the calling from God myself. I had gone along with the steps I had taken up to that point as a matter of obedience.

I announced that I wouldn't take the process any further until I had personally heard from God, which Michael understood and agreed with. He encouraged me to still go on the diocesan's Seeking the Way vocations course, which I had already signed up to. The course was spread out over several Saturdays and evenings and gave plenty of space to talk, to pray together in small groups and to ask lots of questions.[21]

I turned up on the first day of the course feeling quite nervous but praying God would speak to me clearly about the way forward. Claire, who took the course, worked for 3D Coaching,[22] and she warned the group not to worry if, at the end of the course, we felt even more confused!

---

[21] www.stalbans.anglican.org/ministry/vocations (accessed 3rd March 2020).

[22] www.3dcoaching.com (accessed 21st May 2020).

Claire was utterly astonished when I shared with the group towards the end of that first day that God had indeed spoken to me, saying He wanted me to pursue the calling to become a priest. As I had spent time listening to God, I sensed Him saying to me that 'this is the glove [ie the glove of priesthood] I am giving you to put on and it will fit perfectly'. I held on to that phrase for the next six to seven years before I saw it come into full fruition. By hearing from God so early in the course, I was able to relax and enjoy the whole process. Claire assured me that if we were ever to meet up in the future, she would remind me that I was called to be a hospice chaplain and not a parish priest.

When I emailed Claire recently to ask her permission to write about this experience, she willingly agreed. She hoped I would also include the passionate conversation the two of us had had in the kitchen during one of the course lunchbreaks. I was sharing so deeply with Claire that I wasn't aware how physically close I was, brandishing a sharp knife. Claire very carefully took the knife out of my hand and I apologised profusely! We were to meet up at other significant times in the future.

Of course, I quickly contacted Michael to share with him what had happened, and we resumed our regular get-togethers. Michael set me various assignments and encouraged me to embark on an online theological training course to help me gain experience and knowledge on many levels. I valued this whole process with Michael and was pleased it was not rushed. He also encouraged me to start seeing a spiritual director and to take up the discipline of regularly going on a spiritual retreat.

Unsurprisingly, I had to look up the definition of a spiritual director from the London Centre of Spiritual Direction:

> A spiritual director will, in a prayerful atmosphere, help you reflect on your life and experience and help you explore how you might become more open to the movements of the Spirit. Since the earliest days of Christianity people have realised their need to find someone who will walk with them on their journey of faith. [23]

I have greatly valued meeting up with a spiritual director and have truly found the above statement to be true. It has been incredibly useful to take time to meet up with a reflective person of faith who will pray, listen and advise where necessary. No matter how busy my days got, the appointment in my diary to see my director was sacrosanct and was only ever changed if either of us wasn't well or I had been asked to take a funeral.

I took time to explore the different kinds of spiritual retreats on offer as I had never heard of them before Michael suggested making sure they became part of my faith journey. I discovered that people tended to go on one of the following.

Individually guided retreats (known as IGR) can be over any period from three days to a few months. Most people starting out on an IGR go for a shorter length of time to become familiar with the spiritual practice. On

---

[23] lcsd.org.uk/spiritual-direction (accessed 20th January 2020). Permission granted from the London Centre for Spiritual Direction.

average, a week to ten days is usually a comfortable time-out period. While you are on an IGR you would personally meet up each day with a trained spiritual guide. Their remit is to give you space to talk about what is going on for you and what you are hoping to get from the retreat. They will offer you passages of scripture, reflective pieces of poetry or some 'pictures' to spend time with. This kind of retreat tends to be silent and people can come together after breakfast and before supper for a gentle act of worship.

Themed retreats involve being part of a group sharing a creative activity, such as painting or walking, or looking at a specific subject such as leadership. These retreats are much more interactive while still giving you plenty of opportunity for time on your own. Again, there is usually an opportunity to meet up with one of the people leading the group if needed and there will be times of worship each day.

Private retreats are where you spend time on your own in silence, following your own pattern of prayer and meditation, though you can join in with the community's daily times of worship if you wish to. You can usually meet up with a spiritual guide if required, though generally you need to book that opportunity in advance.

Most retreats are held in a residential house and provide a peaceful atmosphere and good, healthy food; many retreat centres are surrounded by the countryside. You can go online and look at the Retreat Association website[24] to find more details of retreat places near you.

---

[24] www.retreats.org.uk (accessed 21st May 2020).

You may be thinking as you read this, why is there a need to physically go on a retreat? Surely meeting with God in our own homes and attending church and a house group is enough? What value is there in going to a retreat centre? Well, if we take the example of knowing how important physical exercise is for our minds and bodies, we realise trying to do exercise on our own can be tough to maintain. There are advantages to physically going to a gym or to an exercise class, where we can be supported and encouraged by others. The same concept can be equally true in looking after our spiritual well-being. Of course, going to church and to a house group is great, but there is something uniquely special about taking concentrated time to come away from the business and pressures of our daily lives.

Over the years I have had many discussions with friends and colleagues about the value of going on retreats. While writing my book I asked several of them for their permission to include their specific feedback, which they gladly agreed to. About half of the people I contacted had attended a retreat and 50% of those are not involved in full-time Christian work. As I think about all the retreats I have attended, most of the other people attending came from ordinary walks of life. My best friend, Sue, shared her initial misgivings on attending a retreat:

> I had always been someone for whom spending time at peace with God's world was considered 'a bit of a waste of time'. I began to learn how to develop the gentle side of me and realised there was so much more to life than 'doing' and 'making'.

And even in those, I could understand better God's continual guidance and love.

I think there is another misconception that spiritual retreats are only for people who generally work abroad for missionary organisations or work full-time in a church or Christian organisation in the United Kingdom.

Lorna stated how she valued 'leaving normal life behind for a couple of days to have time to reflect on what was going on in my life and how I could become more aware or tuned into the presence of God in my daily life'.

Andrew explained how:

> a silent retreat creates space to breathe again and slow down. A new rhythm can be explored through the pattern of worship. Retreating from everyday life into a thin space where God's presence is tangible. Meeting God unexpectedly where our defence mechanisms are lower and the 'real you' is present.

The main reasons why some of my friends hadn't attended a retreat ranged from being too busy, unsure where best to go, lacking confidence, fear of it being 'too Anglican', 'not my cup of tea', probably should have, never thought about going on one, fearing it would make them uncomfortable, preferred to spend time with God either in a garden or in a chapel, could have prayer ministry at church if needed, not felt the need at the moment, having mature Christian friends who challenge them, fearful of taking time out, and one person said, 'That's for holy people!' All these comments are perfectly understandable and need addressing by those who organise retreats and by those of us who have benefited from taking time out on retreat, as we share our experiences.

Some people may not be able to financially afford going on a retreat, and it is useful to know that many retreat centres have bursaries available to assist in this situation. Understandably, some folks may feel embarrassed in taking up this opportunity, but people have donated to these bursaries to enable others to attend.

Going on a silent retreat may, at first, feel daunting and nerve-racking. Going on a themed retreat may be a better way to start, or, equally, going on a quiet day can help to break down any anxieties. Ruth shared her thoughts on attending a themed retreat: 'Time and space to spend in the beautiful gardens; the mixture of spiritual and time spent with others on the retreat.'

I can imagine people wondering how they would use the time set aside, and what if they don't feel God is speaking to them? Reminding ourselves that it is God who does the leading and enjoys His children spending time with Him, and that He does so from a place of love, will hopefully ease some of those understandable anxieties. Another friend, Maureen, appreciated 'the quiet; being with like-minded people, the time for myself and the opportunity to get used to being with myself without feeling a sense of guilt'.

Many of us fear silence, for varied reasons; for me it was associated with difficult childhood memories. Whatever our fears are, we need to remember God knows and understands. He gently and patiently waits for us to take His hand, which is always offered to us, and to start out on this new journey with Him one step at a time. He will never rush us. God is more than capable of transforming our fears of silence into joys!

You may feel concerned by the amount of free time you suddenly find yourself with, especially if you have come away from a demanding job, a busy family life and many other commitments. Recognising that retreat places have a natural rhythm to their days will hopefully help to break down fears. Meals are always at set times, so they can be a natural help to break up your day into sections. Depending on whether you are a morning person or a night owl, you may wish to go for a walk before breakfast or crawl out of bed just in time for the bell to tell you that food is ready! As you mix the day up with gentle walks, praying, snoozes, reading and gentle creative exercises, you will find the time goes by quickly and you start to relax into a different rhythm.

Michael shared what he valued about attending a retreat:

> To be present while the community went about its normal life of prayer; simply the place and space to slow down, to take stock, to do some unhurried reading and praying, to walk and to observe. I suppose you could even say to stretch all the muscles, physical, mental and spiritual.

Finding the right place and the right kind of retreat to suit our personalities is essential in creating the best environment to hear God in a more focused manner. It is essential to have someone you trust to talk to about the experiences you may have while on retreat. It is equally important to pray before, during and after the retreat for

God's protection upon you. You may find things get stirred up inside you and it is vital to go at a pace that works best for you and keeps you safe. Your mental, physical and spiritual well-being need to stay in balance. I could never have imagined meeting God in the way He has so generously opened my heart, mind and soul to such a depth of His intimate love and awesomeness while on retreat.

I took up both of Michael's suggestions concerning a spiritual director and going on retreat as I recognised the importance of building solid foundations within me. I was fully aware of embarking on the important and serious calling into becoming an Anglican priest. To this day I have continued with both disciplines and find them to be of immense value and channels for God to continue His healing work within me.

Another element in the discerning process included an interview with an appointed diocesan psychiatrist, which Michael and I both knew wouldn't be easy. Their role understandably was to assess my mental and emotional fitness and suitability to be eligible for the priesthood. I had confided some details of my background with Michael and he knew I had undertaken extensive counselling. The interview was rigorous, and I cannot say I was relaxed, but I answered the questions as openly as possible. When Michael received the report back from the psychiatrist, he went through it with me, but very wisely said he wasn't going to give me a copy of it. He knew I would go through it with a fine-tooth comb and probably brood on some of the more negative aspects of it. Michael reassured me that there was nothing in the feedback from the psychiatrist that gave him any concerns.

One of the required components to becoming ordained as a priest involved being confirmed so I embarked on attending a series of confirmation classes at my local church, which led to being confirmed at St Albans Abbey. As much as I liked the beauty of the Abbey, I didn't find the process beforehand easy. My decision to profess my faith as a new Christian through adult baptism had meant so much to me, and I honestly did not feel the same way going through the confirmation classes or during the service. However, I knew I had to obey the necessary prerequisites. My lovely friend, Sue, had to put up with my grizzles as we walked up the hill to the Abbey for the confirmation event!

Michael decided that I was ready for the next stage of the ordination process. He wrote to the bishop, who gave me the green light to attend a Bishop's Advisory Panel (BAP). This took place in Ely over a three-day period and consisted of in-depth interviews with four different people. Their role was to discern if my calling was indeed correct and whether they could recommend me to go forward for training. I was acutely aware that they were observing all the interactions going on throughout the group sessions where we were given different tasks to work through, as well as during mealtimes.

I was remarkably calm over those few days at Ely; I was totally honest with the panel of interviewers, clearly stating that I felt called to hospice chaplaincy in order to avoid any misconceptions further down the line. I believed the BAP process was an essential part of testing my calling and understood the importance of the ongoing checking out to see if this was the correct way forward. As the conference ended and I returned home, I clearly remember the words from Paul's letter to the Ephesians coming to mind as I got out of my car:

> And you also were included in Christ when you heard the message of truth, the gospel of your salvation. When you believed, you were marked in him with a seal, the promised Holy Spirit.
> (Ephesians 1:13)

I felt a significant change had occurred within me during the time at Ely, even though at that stage I didn't know the outcome of the BAP. I normally would have been very withdrawn in a strange place with a considerable number of other people; never mind knowing I was being observed! Those words, 'marked in him with a seal', from the letter to the Ephesians, are probably the best way to describe the sense of God giving me the confidence to believe in His calling on my life in a new way.

A few weeks later I received a letter from the bishop saying I had passed the BAP panel. I could now begin the search for the right theological college to embark on my theological training.

My initial hope was to continue working at the hospice in Watford and to do my theological training part-time. However, another major crisis exploded at the hospice which caused me a huge amount of stress, and I had to take some time off from the situation. I felt like I was in the middle of a tug-of-war, being pulled in all directions as the crisis unfortunately deepened. I contacted Claire from 3D Coaching, whom I had met at the vocations course, for some advice, and the hospice agreed to pay for me to work with one of her colleagues. This was the first time I personally encountered the huge benefits of coaching and I found the process both challenging and invigorating. I didn't physically meet the lady who coached me; we agreed to talk on the telephone for an hour at a time for six sessions which were spread out over several months.

Before we even began the coaching, I had to do a fair amount of preparation in relation to the following question:

> What habits/activities/thought processes do you believe need to be dropped, simplified or let go of, in order to truly move forward, quickly? Where are you most irresponsible?[25]

I recognised I was carrying too much baggage and history concerning the hospice. I had spent so much time and energy firefighting, caretaking, bailing people out and crisis managing at a high cost to myself. The clinical staff looked to me to lead them in knowing the best way to voice their concerns over where the hospice was at. I had taken this request on very carefully, knowing how fine a tightrope I would be walking and continually expressing the fact that I couldn't do this alone. They had supported me, but it had meant taking on a lone role which had taken its toll on me personally. The management team of five was now reduced to two and accentuated the personal feelings of being on my own, alongside a deep sense of loss for the staff.

The other question I was asked was, 'What motivates you?' I shared:

---

[25] www.3dcoaching.com (accessed 6th July 2020).

My walk with Jesus, cherishing the intimacy I now have with Him. Praying with a very good friend and enjoying the level of honesty we have with each other. Seeing how Jesus uses me no matter how weak I am, and enjoying being His channel. Being a part of the hospice team and seeing what a difference the clinical staff make to people who are dying and their families – wanting therefore to support the team in whatever way I can to lessen some of the intensity they go through almost on a daily basis.

The coaching sessions were incredibly useful, and I concluded I needed to step away from the predicament and to resign from the hospice. It was an exceptionally difficult decision to make, and I was in anguish over the feelings of letting other staff down, who had looked to me to solve the crisis, but it was not possible. I recall spending hours walking around my local park and praying for wisdom as to how I was going to handle the likely fallout once people heard of my decision to resign. Emotions ran high and I heard through the grapevine that staff had signed a petition urging the hospice trustees to step in to avoid me having to leave. Michael continued to support me throughout this stressful period, and on one of our get-togethers he announced we needed chocolate, which we enjoyed on the way to a repair shop where he had to pick up his bicycle!

We talked at length during the car journey and he instigated an interview with the bishop, who was equally understanding. I still hoped to embark on my theological training part-time and took on several temporary jobs once I finished at the hospice, hoping that could still happen. What I hadn't expected were the bishop's closing words to me as our time together came to an end: 'Stop messing around and go and do your theological training full-time!'

The idea of attending college full-time was a whole different ball game! Alarm bells were immediately going off inside me, as I didn't feel I was intelligent enough to consider this challenge. Part-time training was a much safer prospect on all levels! Full-time study would mean leaving Watford, which had been such an important place of refuge to me and where I had put down solid, healthy roots. I would have to sell my home, which was an even bigger wrench, and again had been so instrumental in many unspoken healing ways. Friends had bought the house I was living in as an investment and I was able to rent it from them until I could afford to start paying a mortgage. Then they generously allowed me to buy a percentage of the house from them. The house had become a major emotional security for me. I would be leaving good friends behind and I even grizzled at the prospect of leaving church!

With very mixed feelings I started to research theological colleges, which I mainly carried out online. The only college that felt tolerable on all levels was St John's in Bramcote, on the outskirts of Nottingham. With a high degree of trepidation, I went to one of their visiting days with my good friend Sue. We both sensed throughout the day that this was the best place for me, and I reluctantly started the process of applying and being interviewed for the Diploma in Theological Ministry course. I didn't feel capable of undertaking a degree course and it was important I stayed where possible in the few remaining comfort zones, as so many others were being taken away from me! I was successful in the interview, signifying lots of changes were looming.

Putting my home up for sale and going through the fraught procedure of negotiating a fair price was as stressful as people warn you about. There were times Sue had to gently and courageously remind me why I was needing to sell my home when I overreacted to 'silly offers'. I recognised some of my emotional frailties were coming to the surface and causing me a high degree of concern, so I contacted my counsellor in London. I valued being able to work through some of those fears and frailties over several sessions which helped me to calm down and to prepare myself for a new journey.

9
Attending Theological College

I was fortunate to be offered one of the few residential flats at college and moved in while my house was still slowly going through the selling stages. I cannot say I was happy, but I knew it was important to make the most of the next two years. The first few months were quite emotional, with the combination of the pain of the completion of selling my house, the pain of leaving Watford and digesting all the new changes I had embarked on. I was conscious of how often tears were being shed – from someone who thought it would never happen!

I sensed God was encouraging me to use the years at college in a joyful way, which would involve continually praying about the fears that I sensed were holding me back with each new experience I was going through. I was also reminded that as one of His children, I always had an open invitation to hold God's hand, and how I had been adopted by Him. Here was yet another indicator of spending time at His banquet hall and drinking in all I needed.

The gift of adoption

Throughout the Bible we are given countless references to God adopting us as His children, from the early laws found in Deuteronomy[26] through to Paul's letter to the church in Ephesus. The apostle Paul understood the gift God had given His people and encouraged groups of Christians not to forget their inheritance:

> For he chose us in him before the creation of the world to be holy and blameless in his sight. In love he predestined us for adoption to sonship through Jesus Christ, in accordance with his pleasure and will.
> (Ephesians 1:4-5)

God offers His children the gift of adoption, knowing it may not be easy for some of us to accept it initially. Trusting God in those places of vulnerability where we may feel more like an orphan rather than an adopted child takes time and patience. It is vitally important to first work through the strata of loss and other difficult emotions before we can fully embrace accepting God's gift. If we don't go through this process, the foundation will not prove to be solid enough. The pain of acknowledging and facing the difficult truth of being unloved by my parents who brought me into the world ran incredibly deep. God is fully aware of that depth of pain, and I believe finds many ways to compensate for those losses and suffering.

Reading Psalm 139 was fundamental in personally recognising God's gift of calling on my life. I have spent so

---

[26] See Deuteronomy 10:18.

much time meditating again and again on the many sections of this psalm, looking at it with other biblical translations to gain different insights while thinking about God adopting me as His child. These specific verses strike a deep chord in me:

> For you created my inmost being;
> you knit me together in my mother's womb.
> I praise you because I am fearfully and wonderfully made;
> your works are wonderful,
> I know that full well.
> My frame was not hidden from you
> when I was made in the secret place,
> when I was woven together in the depths of the earth.
> Your eyes saw my unformed body;
> all the days ordained for me were written in your book
> before one of them came to be.
> (Psalm 139:13-16)

Accepting God's gift of adoption enabled me to ask some difficult questions I had never allowed myself to face before, or to trust God with. I needed to ask why God had permitted me to be born into an abusive environment, where I was clearly not wanted. The hidden questions of 'Why did those awful things happen to me and why didn't God intervene and stop the abuse?' had silently haunted me. As I learned to trust God, I was able to recognise I didn't need to protect Him from what felt like unspoken, disloyal thoughts. God is well and truly big enough to hear my questions, which in His eyes were vitally important. In return, God was able to work at an inner, supernatural level within me. It has taken many years to finally believe that He was with me during those years of abuse. Without His presence I fully recognise I would not have survived. I can look back at a few incidences which I now acknowledge were God-inspired.

I remember as a child reading a book about Gladys Aylward (though I have no recollection of the title), who had been a missionary in China. In the late 1930s China had been invaded by Japan and Miss Aylward led almost 100 children over the mountains to safety as she feared for their lives.[27]

I have no idea where I got the book from or how I managed to keep it hidden from my parents. I know I read it many times and I sense it would have given me courage and fortitude not to give up.

I acknowledge I was saved from potential death on many occasions, given how many times my mother appeared to attempt to drown me. I am very aware that humanly speaking, I could have easily suffered major mental health problems as a result of my upbringing, which thankfully hasn't occurred. I fully recognise now that in the absence of any humanity, I was not alone; God was present.

God's gift of adoption can be eloquently summed up with these precious words from the prophet Isaiah: 'See, I have engraved you on the palms of my hands' (Isaiah

---

[27] Gladys Aylward's life story was made into a film entitled *The Inn of the Sixth Happiness* in 1958 (20th Century Fox) based on the book by Alan Burgess, *The Small Woman* (London: Pan, 1957).

49:16). Personally, I know without doubt that I am a child adopted by the Father, and this alone gives me an incredible foundation, framework and inheritance on which to base all I do.

I was relieved that Michael continued to support me during my time at college and looked forward to his visits. I committed myself to studying as well as possible and ensured I completed my assignments on time. I struggled being around so many people, as I had been comfortable spending a great deal of time on my own in Watford. Many people complained of feeling deskilled while at college, but I didn't find that as I looked for different opportunities to pastorally encourage others. A small group of us decided to cook a meal for all the support staff who worked behind the scenes at college, and we had a great evening with them.

The television programme *Deal or No Deal*, hosted by Noel Edmunds, was shown at a time when many of the residential students were finishing lectures. My flat became the social hub where folks gathered around the television, drinking coffee and boisterously taking part. It was a great way to unwind and to relax for a short period of time.

I was given permission to attend a pastoral care course at the local hospice near to the college. I thoroughly enjoyed the opportunity to attend the course and appreciated being back in the hospice world, albeit briefly. Unbeknown to me, this wouldn't be the last contact I had with the person who led the training course.

I was introduced to a valuable tool, Lectio Divina, during my time at college, when the principal spent some time teaching and giving students time to practise the discipline. There are different ways you can use this resource and it is well worth prayerfully practising them at different times, either individually or within a group. The first is to read a passage of Scripture out loud several times, asking God to speak to you. As that happens, it is important not to rush the process and to stay with the word or phrase. It is useful to write down what you believe God is saying to you. You may want to stay at that place or continue with the passage, repeating the same process.

Another way of using Lectio Divina was used by the college principal who would start a teaching session praying for God to meet with the students individually and then read out loud a parable from one of the Gospels. We were encouraged to imagine ourselves as one of the participants in the parable, to take in the surroundings and the atmosphere and to allow God to personally speak to us as the story unfolded. We were free to share what we had experienced during the session if we wished to.

I enjoyed learning about this discipline and realised how using Lectio Divina can be a powerful tool whereby God is able to speak in a deeper way. However, it is always important to test out these experiences to ensure they align with biblical principles, as our minds are human vessels! Talking through what we may feel God has said to us through these encounters with a trusted, wise person is essential. You may wish to look at the Bible Society's summary of this precious and profound resource, as it offers a free download as a guide to using the Lectio Divina approach.[28]

When I started to use Lectio Divina on my own, I sensed Jesus was encouraging me to create a 'safe place' in my mind where I could meet with Him at an inner level. Details and choice mattered in this process, as Jesus knew how important it was for me to feel safe and encouraged me to ask for things I wanted within this place. I imagined a cave that was lit with myriads of candles to provide warmth and adequate light. Choosing a royal blue snuggly blanket was a must, which many times I felt Jesus gently wrap around me when I most needed to feel His protection. It was in this precious place that I began to talk to Jesus at an intimate level, as I learned to trust Him and become the child He called and invited me to be. I enjoyed the delights of experiencing this new intimate relationship with Him. Sharing these encounters with my spiritual director was an important element; to check that the experiences were godly based and that my mind wasn't taking me on some wild goose chase!

More frailties emerged during my time at college and I realised I needed to undertake some further counselling. Given I had so little knowledge of Anglicanism, I had volunteered to join the team of sacristans who helped to set up the communion table for the weekly evening service held in the college chapel. I reckoned this would be a useful role to become familiar with in readiness for becoming a curate. One of the sacristan tasks involved consuming any spare bread and wine left over from the

[28] www.biblesociety.org.uk/explore-the-bible/lectio-divina (accessed 15th January 2020).

communion service. Unfortunately, as I did this, it provoked such an explosive reaction inside me, linked to my past, that I had to withdraw from being a volunteer. However, I knew I couldn't ignore the strong reactions within me as I would face the same problem further down the road in a church environment.

One of the ongoing difficulties of living with all the damage inflicted upon me by my parents and brother was never knowing when fears and difficult memories would get triggered. There were many times I despaired at having to face yet more 'inner demons'. I longed for an end to what I regarded as introspective navel-gazing, but knew, at the same time, I was being incredibly harsh on myself with those judgements. It also meant being vulnerable with new people as I sought help for God's healing concerning the reaction I had had over the bread and wine. I knew it was linked to those awful times when I had been forced to eat soggy bread as a child. I also recognised there were times when God needed to carry out a spiritual inner healing, as no amount of talking would resolve such emotional damage.

I never felt forced by God to embark on yet another round of healing when it was needed. He always waited for me to agree to addressing the frailties within me when they were being triggered. I always had choices: I could attempt to ignore what was going on inside me, or I could take another deep breath and allow God to enact another piece of healing work. It didn't mean I relished the process, as I knew it would be deeply painful. With a heavy heart I approached the principal of the college and requested some help.

God used that incident to initiate more healing on a spiritual level, but it was physically and emotionally gruelling. I was given permission not to attend lectures as the healing prayer sessions I undertook over the next few months left me exhausted. During one of those sessions I was given a prophetic word of knowledge[29] about my future ministry where God would use me to 'meet the needs of the marginalised people'. God is so incredibly gracious; when I was at my weakest, He would encourage and help me to hold on to His promises.

Halfway through my theological course, I chose to undertake the required two-week placement at Burrswood, which was described as a Christian hospital and a place of healing. It was based at Groombridge in Tunbridge Wells, Kent. I went to Burrswood with the specific aim of wanting the experience to shape my future ministry. I was keen to see how an interdisciplinary team worked together in bringing about a holistic approach to healing. I desired to gain more experience in listening to God and praying in different situations. I was interested to see how the staff personally looked after themselves given the intense nature of their work. I also looked forward to exploring how the different types of services complemented the specific work the chaplains were engaged in. Burrswood was set in beautiful surroundings and it was a sheer pleasure to be able to walk around the grounds each day, taking the time to pray and reflect during the two weeks I was there.

---

[29] A word of knowledge or prophetic word is a word from God about something we cannot naturally know. See 1 Corinthians 12:1-11.

Looking back, I was grateful how God had prepared me concerning my placement at Burrswood during the months beforehand. Going through the deep process of inner healing enabled me to fully engage in the pastoral ministry the chaplains were involved in. The placement was not an observation; it was a full-blooded, hands-on experience with minimal supervision. I prayed with and walked alongside several people who had come to Burrswood seeking God's healing. I led a series of devotional services and was part of the team who ministered to people at the end of the weekly communion service.

It was important that I already had the confidence in what I believed God was equipping me for in the longer term, not in any arrogant way but in a quiet, calm, assured manner. I came away from the Burrswood placement knowing that style of ministry of being on the fringes was something I relished and wanted to be fully engaged in. I was saddened to discover that Burrswood has now closed owing to financial difficulties.

The next challenge I faced came as I approached the end of my course at college. Even though I steadfastly knew my calling was to be a hospice chaplain, I accepted I had to follow the usual Anglican route of undertaking a curacy. I wasn't looking forward to the prospect of spending the next four years wholly in a church environment.

There was a standard procedure at college that needed to be followed in seeking the right place to undertake the curacy placement. You were offered two opportunities within your own diocese on the advice of the director of ordinands. You were then free to apply anywhere else in the country if you didn't accept one of these opportunities, or were not accepted.

When I met up with Michael to discuss a way forward for me, he was incredibly honest and said he didn't feel there was a suitable place within the St Albans diocese. He knew how much hospice ministry was at the centre of my being and did not want that to be stifled. Despite his concerns he did his very best to search out any possible place for me within the diocese and I so appreciated yet again his support and care for me. Michael was spot on in his assessment and I was therefore released by the diocese to look elsewhere.

I strongly felt the only way I was going to manage the next four years was to have hospice chaplaincy as part of my curacy. That requirement became part of my discussions with prospective training incumbents. If my request was turned down, I felt I had no choice but to withdraw from the opportunity of having a curacy in any church I was looking at. This was by no means easy. Ninety-nine per cent of people attending theological college feel called to be an Anglican priest in a parish ministry role. I often sensed during my time at college that I was the odd one out.

I also recognised there was a fear factor in looking at a place in a church environment. As I spent time praying over these concerns, I sensed God ask me two questions. Did I feel called to be an ordained priest? My answer was affirmative. The second question was, did I feel called to be an ordained priest in a parish? My answer was a clear no.

I recognised how being in an up-front role terrified and horrified me. I was so much more comfortable being in a behind-the-scenes role, which chaplaincy allows. I realised I had only accepted God's call to be ordained as an intellectual and rational exercise. Emotionally, I realised, to my dismay, that I didn't trust God, as I feared He would take the calling away from me. As I recognised those anxieties were linked to deep-rooted childhood experiences, I sought prayer from others over these revelations. As I was prayed for, I sensed Jesus physically scooping out all the poison from my inner being concerning these apprehensions. I visualised Jesus replacing the poison with His healing love which permeated every part of me – my veins, my arteries, my muscles, etc. It was a powerful experience that has stayed with me.

I was offered a curacy in Norfolk but regretfully turned it down when my request for hospice chaplaincy was declined. My decision did not go down well at college and I was told I had declined the best curacy offer available in the country. I felt I was being labelled as a 'rebel' and agonised about the best way forward. I was grateful for the support I received from other students who knew me well. One of the tutors who had briefly tried to teach me Greek in the early months of college life lived in the flat below mine. When she heard about my predicament, she went out on a limb for me in openly backing my request. She came to see me in my apartment one afternoon to express her support and gently held me as I sobbed in helpless frustration.

Michael was, as always, still supporting me, even though officially he didn't have to, as I had been released by the diocese. Of course, Sue also continued to offer me her care and encouragement on many levels and managed to come with me on the visits to different parishes. Out of the blue, Michael contacted me and said he had found a possible curacy for me to look at which would involve some definite hospice chaplaincy. My hopes were raised as I went to visit the area, discovered where the hospice was and met with the vicar. The visit went extremely well, and I was excited at the possibility of thinking that at last I had found the place to undertake my curacy.

A few weeks later I went back with Sue to attend the morning service at the church. My heart sank as throughout the service I clearly sensed God disclose this was not the place for me. I was unable to make eye contact with the vicar and it took me quite a while to be able to speak to Sue as we sat in the car afterwards. I was devastated and disappointed by this latest setback. I felt I was left in no man's land and feared whether I would be able to get ordained. I knew I had to hang in there, trusting that God would provide, and not panic. It was hard, though, as so many other students around me were talking about moving on, making plans, and I couldn't join in with them. I prayed with two of my college friends and the words I had heard during the vocations course came back loud and clear that my ministry would fit perfectly, like a glove, and God would provide.

As time marched on and my options were becoming fewer, I applied for a curacy at a village church within the Oxford diocese. During my conversations with the parish priest, he heard my request and agreed to ensure that I would have an opportunity to explore hospice chaplaincy during my curacy training. As a result, I agreed to embark on my curacy there.

10
Life as a Curate

My time at college came to an end and I prepared to move to Oxford with very mixed feelings. I firstly had to prepare for the formal service where I would become an ordained deacon, and it was important to put aside all my uncertainties surrounding the next four years and to focus on the immediate road ahead. Going through the service at Oxford cathedral where I was officially ordained as a deacon was a powerful and humbling experience. The parish priest, who was now my training incumbent, sat behind me and I could hear his strong voice during the worship and the prayer times.

I had not invited anyone from my family to this event as they would be so confused as to why I was being ordained a deacon during the first year and then ordained as a priest the following year. I had decided I would only invite them to the second service, which was scheduled to go ahead in Banbury. I also recognised that wherever possible, I did not disclose much to my family about my present life as there were still childhood fears around the idea that they would do something to ruin it for me.

A new chapter started, and those next four years of my life were very up and down. On the plus side I thoroughly enjoyed the training relationship with my incumbent. I learned so much from him during my time in Oxford; his humbleness, honesty and servanthood as well as his great sense of humour all helped me to trust him. He was incredibly gracious, patient and tolerant when he realised how little I knew about Anglicanism and all that was involved in being an Anglican priest. I can honestly say that if it wasn't for him, I would have thrown in the towel during that period.

Four months into my curacy I asked my incumbent where he saw me in my role. He talked of seeing a huge internal struggle going on, and wondered where God and I would end up in the process! He recognised how I was feeling deskilled and stripped of all I had previously associated with a job. He acknowledged how this was a lonely and uncomfortable path to be on, but also recognised my willingness to be open to whatever came along, and to let God be my God in a deeply vulnerable way. He talked about the differences between a curate and a parish priest and advised me not to take on the battles of running a church. Instead he encouraged me to keep focusing on prayer, pastoral care, liturgy, preaching and relating to the community.

I struggled with many different aspects associated with the curacy process. I wasn't comfortable living in such a large house, which was generously supplied with the role, and I recognised I preferred smaller dwellings. I missed having my own home at a deeper inner level where the fragile part of me desperately needed security. I wasn't confident being in an up-front position and I certainly knew preaching was not my natural gift. It was incredibly daunting putting a sermon together, knowing there were many academics in the congregation, alongside several retired priests! They were, however, always very generous towards me. In fact, they could not understand why I did not wish to pursue parish ministry and made their feelings clear to me during my years with them! My struggles had absolutely nothing to do with the lovely people who attended the church; they were incredibly supportive throughout my time there.

It was important to keep working at being myself, to hold on to the calling I had clearly been given and not to be boxed in by well-meaning people concerning my future. I also recognised that when it came to my priesting ceremony less than a year away, I would be standing up in front of my family not as a timid, damaged child running away, but rather as a child of God, constantly being transformed through His grace and mercy.

There were times when parts of my childhood were triggered as a result of where I was physically living, which strongly reminded me of where I had been brought up. Continually accepting and embracing all the fragile, fractured parts of me was a struggle, especially when I felt those triggers came close to paralysing my everyday living. I recognised afresh how healing was not about a magic wand being waved over those damaged years of my childhood. Yes, I had an overall healing, but the walk of intimacy Jesus calls me to is an everyday one which at times brings fresh challenges. I got frustrated and angry about never getting to a place within me where dealing with my past was completed. Of course, I knew that wasn't going to happen, but I still wished the inner gremlins would disappear!

I greatly valued Lectio Divina in my quiet times with God and how He continued to give me 'pictures' to help me in my inner walk with Him. As I expressed my anger to God about these ongoing frustrations of facing the unpredictability of different emotions being triggered within me from my childhood, I sensed Him ask, was I afraid that my frailties would swamp me, and was I able to stay in that place of woundedness to be His servant?

I had been spending time reading the passage from Luke 8 where the woman who had been suffering from internal bleeding for years heard that Jesus was going to be in her neighbourhood. Despite the cultural taboo she knew she was subjected to, the woman bravely joined the crowd awaiting Jesus' arrival. As He passed close to her, she reached out and touched the hem of His cloak and was immediately healed (Luke 8:42-48). As I meditated on these words, I found myself saying to Jesus, 'I don't just want one touch from You.'

As He drew me aside, He gently asked, 'What do you need?'

My mind went into freefall; I was all over the place as words jumbled around in my head. I didn't know how to answer coherently. After a few minutes I was able to reply, 'I want to have an inner home, a place where I know I belong, a place where all the different parts of me come together.' Jesus asked me to explain more and I said how the 'survival' part of me had taken precedence again since moving to Oxford. I went through the good experiences I had valued towards the end of my time at Watford, and how I had come off my 'remote emotional island'. I moved on to talk about college and how I had experienced and greatly appreciated the depths of healing that had transpired during my time there. I ended this honest conversation by asking Jesus why He did all of that, to then bring me to this place where I was now at, a place where I felt more alone, more constrained, more deskilled and inwardly unsafe. In Watford I had had a home; here I felt homeless. I grieved for in-depth, real, honest, two-way conversations. I missed being in a multidisciplinary team and I missed my friends.

I knew this wasn't about questioning my calling or doubting I was in the right place, or about a physical location called 'home'. I was aware that all the safety nets had been stripped away for an even deeper piece of healing work to be enacted. Most of what I was 'naturally' good at had been taken away. I recognised afresh how, ever since I had left home, I had worked, often in a need to forget my background, and had run away from all that 'home' had represented. The place I was now living in was a constant reminder of my family home as it was located on a housing estate with a high degree of poverty and vulnerable children living in dysfunctional family units. It was here where God needed to do further surgery – and I was unimpressed, to put it politely!

This inner crisis continued for a good three months, taking me to a place of lowness and depression. I knew enough to face what was going on, to name the conflicting feelings and to allow God to bring me through the storm I was going through, at the right pace, as it could not be rushed. It was a hard position to be in, waking up each day feeling lost, empty and alone; it felt like an endurance test. Some of the disciplines of being a priest also triggered my emotional frailties. Learning how to be reflective threw me into too much silence that echoed those times of being locked away as a child. I missed the noise and vibrancy of my former workplaces. I felt straitjacketed; it seemed like

I had to let go of the livelier elements of my personality. I felt I was back on a remote 'island', but this time not of my choosing.

Despite my inner weaknesses and frailties, I sensed Jesus being with me. I knew I was not alone, and He was giving me the strength and courage to 'hang in there'. As tears finally came to the surface, I was reminded of so many verses that spoke about God's love surrounding me, how He had known me from the point of conception and how I belonged to Him. I grasped hold of three key passages throughout this crisis:

> He reached down from on high and took hold of me;
> he drew me out of deep waters …
> He brought me out into a spacious place;
> he rescued me because he delighted in me
> (Psalm 18:16,19)

> For I am convinced that neither death nor life, neither angels nor demons, neither the present nor the future, nor any powers, neither height nor depth, nor anything else in all creation, will be able to separate us from the love of God that is in Christ Jesus our Lord.
> (Romans 8:38-39)

> And I pray that you, being rooted and established in love, may have power, together with all the Lord's holy people, to grasp how wide and long and high and deep is the love of Christ.
> (Ephesians 3:17-18)

The gift of belonging

One of the most profound treasures I have received from God from His banquet hall of divine love is the gift of belonging. If we haven't been fortunate enough to grow up in a stable and loving environment, we will probably not have acquired a strong sense of belonging. Society puts huge pressures on us to belong, though that usually means to conform! It is so much harder to step back and decide not to go with the crowd mentality and to be the person we are called to be. Huge institutions are not able to give much space for individuality, so from an early age, youngsters are expected to conform through the school system, irrespective of their abilities or social skills. Teenagers can get caught up in 'hero worship' of their favourite pop artist or sports star, never mind all the complexities around social media or wearing the 'right gear'.

As we start out on a career path, it can be so easy to be seduced into our identity, our sense of belonging revolving around a job. Parents can get caught up in the trap of their identity being incredibly focused on their children, which can lead to unhealthy relationships and difficulties around the 'empty nest' syndrome when offspring leave the family home.

If we haven't acquired the healthy social skills needed to work out where we belong, we may make the mistake of looking at those around us. We may feel we need to imitate their behaviour to gain that sense of inclusion. We regularly hear on the news of a gang mentality ruling housing estates and the surrounding streets and how youngsters are coerced into violent acts to gain that all-important badge of belonging. It's unlikely that any of these understandable attempts at belonging will help us to gain an inner sense of satisfaction, though, and they often have the opposite effect and accentuate that emptiness within our beings. This sense of dissatisfaction can lead us on to more difficult and dangerous paths. We may be tempted to look to external substances to deaden the emptiness or loneliness, like drugs, sex or alcohol. These in themselves will, of course, lead us into an even greater false sense of belonging.

Personal temperaments will also play a factor in how or where we belong; introverts and extroverts have very different spiritual, emotional and physical requirements. It is essential that we all work out the elements we need to ensure we find that right balance of belonging, so that we don't fall into the trap of getting swayed by tempting, quick-fix solutions of fitting in.

Sometimes God's gifts can initially feel like anything but good! They can provoke the very opposite of what they are intended to offer. The gift of belonging has been one of the most difficult and painful concepts for me to pursue and believe that I would ever attain. For most of my life I have felt the opposite of belonging. I haven't felt connected with the people around me; I don't tick as others tick. I have often felt crushed and empty with an overwhelming sense of not belonging anywhere.

This can be a very lonely place, as most people would have little idea of the struggles some of us may be going through in working out where we do, in fact, belong. We rarely share these difficulties for fear of offending those closest to us, as they may justifiably take it the wrong way.

It's fascinating to read through the Gospels about where Jesus' sense of belonging came from. It would have been so easy for Jesus to have allowed His disciples to dictate where He needed to be on a day-to-day basis. He could have easily got caught up in the dangers of delusion by staying in the place of enjoying the shallow worship of the crowds. He might have become totally submerged with the depth of physical, mental, spiritual and emotional needs around Him. He could have allowed His ego to take centre stage. If He had allowed the never-ending needs of all the people to shape His days, Jesus would have quickly found Himself facing burnout. It would have been totally understandable if He had allowed the continual criticism thrown at Him by the Pharisees to undermine the calling He knew God had given Him. At any point in His life, Jesus could have misused the power and authority within Him to 'belong' on a human level.

Jesus didn't do any of the above. Instead we read how there were many times He went off on His own, to pray and to be quiet. He continually stood up to the authorities, refusing to conform to distorted legal viewpoints that resulted in hardship and suffering for the people around Him. He understood what His mission was in the short time He had here, and kept true to His calling. He knew He was greatly loved by His Father, even when He was facing betrayal, torture and, the ultimate, crucifixion, and ending of His life on earth.

Holding on to this precious truth of belonging may, logically, cause conflict in our inner beings. The notion of belonging in a place of holiness where God resides will also uncover those areas within us where we may feel fear and shame. At times that conflict can feel like a raging tumult of mixed emotions, a sense of not feeling worthy enough to dare to believe we belong to God. Our immediate instinct can be one of running away and hiding.

If we are not operating from our own place of belonging, we will come across to others as inauthentic, and we are not being truly ourselves. Many people struggle in their employment because they are not doing what they instinctively feel they have been designed to do and sense an ongoing inner dissatisfaction.

There is a story in the Gospels about a leper falling at Jesus' feet and asking for healing:

> When Jesus came down from the mountainside, large crowds followed him. A man with leprosy came and knelt before him and said, 'Lord, if you are willing, you can make me clean.'
>
> Jesus reached out his hand and touched the man. 'I am willing,' he said. 'Be clean!' Immediately he was cleansed of his leprosy. Then Jesus said to him, 'See that you don't tell anyone. But go, show yourself to the priest and offer the gift Moses commanded, as a testimony to them.' (Matthew 8:1-4)

Jesus knew the leper's sense of belonging was a lonely, insular one through no fault of his own. He was shunned by society because of the nature of his disease; he was suffering physically and fearful of his future. It's likely he would have shut down emotionally at the withdrawal of loved ones no longer demonstrating physical affection to him. To his heart cry for healing, Jesus responded with utter compassion and touched the man, thereby giving him a new sense of belonging as he could re-engage with society.

As I spent time meditating on this passage, I sensed Jesus say to me that once the leper was healed, there was no need for him to stay dressed in rags or to stay as an outcast. But it can be difficult to come away from that role, that box, which others or circumstances have created or enforced on any of us. Personally, the touch of Jesus means I belong, I am understood by Him. Jesus sees beyond what my parents and brother had made me into; the very fact that Jesus meets me at my very worst and loves me is profound. Where the world casts me out, Jesus welcomes me; where I have been dressed in rags, Jesus dresses me in beautiful clothes.

I needed to continually work on being in the new place of healing Jesus has given me, which happens even in the ordinariness of my home and garden. Over the years, there has been a gentle, unspoken restoration process going on in the 'normal' humdrum of looking after my home. I have prayed for God to help me with the gift of creativity and to allow it to flourish in its natural sense in the way I have designed my home.

My inner being needs to be nourished and looked after in a trusting environment. When I crave and ache for a sense of human belonging, I need to return to where I am utterly welcomed. The world will not and is not able to help me in that yearning to belong. Only God can, because He knows and understands my frailties. It has taken a long time to enjoy all I have around me. For too long I would buy things I needed, but it left me feeling empty inside. God's gift of belonging has transformed that emptiness.

One of the advantages of maturing in age is the realisation that I am free to make decisions based around my personality. I no longer subject myself to situations I have previously felt coerced into. For example, going to conferences where huge numbers of people gather has always been excruciatingly difficult for me. Understanding why that is the case is one thing, but then actually stepping back and saying, 'I do not need to put myself through such an ordeal,' is liberating. That is not about avoiding; it is more about knowing who I am and how there are certain things I don't need to fight an ongoing battle about. I am much more comfortable and flourish healthily around small groups of people.

At the start of one new year I wrote in my journal:

> I cherish the joy and outrageous generosity of a love relationship with the Father. I cherish that deep sense of belonging.

What an incredible statement to start the year with! Knowing I belong to God is at the very centre of my being. That promise keeps me secure, balanced and in a healthy place.

Despite the emotional frailties I experienced during my curacy, I greatly valued the freedom my incumbent gave me, and he was a great encourager in trying out new pieces of work. We had a good relationship with the local Methodist deacon, and the two of us worked together on innovative projects, especially as we both lived on the same housing estate. One of the initiatives we collaborated on was to offer support to the staff running a local children's centre. We were asked to put together a reflective short service over a lunchtime for any staff wanting to come along, and we enjoyed meeting with different people. That led on to setting up a social bereavement group at the same centre one evening a week. We both spent quality time with a group of pensioners who were in the throes of moving into new residential accommodation. As they settled into their new premises, we set up a monthly informal communion service.

The church received frequent requests for baptisms, so we designed a new style of service for the families, which they were invited to after the main morning service had finished. Formal organ music was replaced by modern Christian worship and we made use of good Christian children's books alongside the important legal wording for the baptism.

Presiding at the weekly communion services was a profound privilege and took me to a place within myself where honesty with God was paramount. Being open with Him concerning my own frailties allowed me to offer communion to the church family with His grace and mercy. I recall the first time I led an Ash Wednesday service and being totally unprepared for the emotional impact of physically marking a sign of the cross in ashes on people's foreheads, including my incumbent's. Afterwards I shared with him how I was blown away by this act and how, once more, I was reminded of my servanthood to God being the primary factor in all my actions.

I held on to the prospect of embarking on a placement at a nearby hospice. I met up with the chaplain there and arrangements were put in place for me to attend one day a week for six weeks. I was apprehensive as I started on the placement. I was banking so much on getting the green light from God during my time there. I hoped He would clarify that He was still calling me to be a hospice chaplain. Bewilderingly, I didn't get that green light, which threw me into utter confusion; in fact, I didn't hear God at all! I went so far as to deciding over the ensuing weeks that I had no choice but to abandon my dream of becoming a hospice chaplain and to start looking for parish ministry roles. I remember the day I shared this with Sue on one of her visits to me, and I was somewhat surprised at her reaction to my announcement. She burst into tears at what she was hearing, but said very little as she needed space to digest what I was saying.

I could identify with the disciples as to where they were at emotionally after Jesus had died and risen again but was no longer with them. In all the tumult of emotions they went back to their fishing jobs. They felt abandoned; they had given everything up to follow Jesus and now they faced an uncertain future. Holding on to the belief that hospice chaplaincy was my calling for so many years and now thinking I had no choice but to let go of that belief left me grief-stricken and desolate. Like the disciples, I realised trying to turn the clock back to what was familiar was neither healthy nor successful. The seemingly unsuccessful hospice placement had left me with an 'empty net'. I knew without a shadow of doubt I had only embarked on the ordination process, going through theological college and the curacy training as a walk of obedience. The one thing that had kept me going during those years was knowing the ultimate goal of hospice chaplaincy would be realised. I questioned whether I had held on to a past belief which now felt futile and a sense that the 'hospice clothes' no longer fitted me.

Jesus did not leave me on my own, though. As He had stood on the shore waiting for the disciples to return from their fruitless night's fishing, so He did with me. With the safety net of chaplaincy seemingly being removed, all sorts of voices were going around my head. I talked honestly with my incumbent, sharing with him how, as I saw Jesus by the shore, I wanted to ignore Him, to say I'd had enough; I wanted to row off on my own and walk away from it all; there was a sense of stubbornly wanting to dig my heels in. It took time to let go of my stubbornness, anger and resentment before I was able to take up the offer of having breakfast with Jesus by the shore, as He had done with His disciples (John 21:1-14).

Going on retreat for a week in Southampton was a useful interlude and enabled me to stand back and again hold on to God's promises. He continued to be my rock; He was ever-faithful. There was nothing that God could not heal within me. He reminded me that He had seen all that had happened to me as a child and that His Son, Jesus, had given His life so that I 'may have life, and have it to the full' (John 10:10). It was important for me to keep letting go of my survival mechanisms and to hold on to the inheritance God had given me, that will 'never perish … or fade' (1 Peter 1:4). My prayer coming out of that retreat week was, 'May I keep hold of Your inexpressible joy, Lord, which is indeed glorious, Your love which lavishly pours over me and Your grace which is abounding.'

With very mixed feelings I started to apply for jobs as a parish priest; the process took considerable time. It was important to have something sorted before my curacy finished in the early summer months of the following year. I wouldn't have given me either of the two jobs I applied and was interviewed for, as I could not conjure up any enthusiasm for them. I applied for a post as a hospital chaplain on the outskirts of London, again out of a sense of desperation, and was offered the job. I turned it down as I knew very clearly during the informal interview that this position wasn't my calling. I also did not fancy the idea of observing post-mortems, which was strangely part of the job description!

Out of the blue, my spiritual director sent me an advert she had seen concerning a post for a hospice chaplain based in Nuneaton. My initial reaction was one of anger and disbelief! She knew all I had gone through and how I had had to let go of my heart's desire of hospice chaplaincy, so why on earth was she encouraging me to apply for the job? Time had elapsed since the disappointing experience at the local hospice and I now felt able to talk it all through with Sue from a different perspective. She was adamant that I should not have given up my calling to be a hospice chaplain after the placement, but had kept quiet and waited until I was ready to work out what had gone askew during those six weeks.

I recognised several contributing factors that had caused me to have such a negative reaction and to abandon my long-held dream. Shortly before going on the placement, my older sister had been diagnosed with colon cancer. At the time of her diagnosis I wasn't sure if I should delay the arrangement, but I felt I would be OK.

Going on a placement for one day a week was not easy; I didn't have many opportunities to develop any ongoing relationships with the patients. It was a busy inpatient unit and I was left very much to my own devices and lacked confidence to walk into people's rooms, feeling I was cold-calling! Hanging over me during the time was an unspoken pressure that I had to be willing to let go of my dream. Is it any wonder that under those circumstances I had not been able to hear God?

Tentatively, I applied for the role of hospice chaplain in Nuneaton and arranged to go for an informal visit. I was offered an interview and one of the wardens from my training church kindly drove me to the appointment. On our journey back to Oxford I received a phone call from the chair of trustees offering me the job, which I gladly accepted! The chief executive shared with me a few months later that she had wanted me on board because I had made her laugh during the interview!

During the last few months of my curacy, the diocese sent all their curates on a course to help them with putting a CV together, how to sell themselves on an application form and tips on how to handle an interview. The course was run by Claire and other members of her team from 3D Coaching. Even though I had formally accepted the hospice job and had a starting date, I was still required to attend the course. When we gathered altogether for supper on the first evening, Claire took one look at me and asked, 'Why have the lights gone out in you?' I hadn't seen her for about seven years, but she immediately knew something had died inside me. In many ways, that was the extra confirmation I needed to hear that parish ministry was not my calling!

I don't know how, but Claire and her team also picked up that I was not part of the curacy group. Because I had come into the diocese as an outsider, I had found it very difficult to break into an established cluster when we got together for other training events. Claire and her team took it upon themselves, without saying anything to me, to look after me during the conference, which I found very touching. She also decided I didn't need to do the work the other curates were assigned to do as the job at the hospice in Nuneaton had been confirmed. She encouraged me to spend the day on my own and gave me a book called *The Path*,[30] which had a number of exercises to work through, to help me to figure out what my personal mission statement was in readiness for my new role at the hospice. It was to prove a very powerful experience and I hold on to that mission statement to this day. As I worked through the specific exercises, I concluded that my mission statement involved 'finding opportunities to create, to delight and to enable healing'. My core value linked with this statement focused around 'restoration for all'.

I was immensely grateful to Claire for her wisdom and insights. I came away from that conference re-energised and excited at finally being able to fulfil my calling to be a hospice chaplain. I was very thankful to God for engineering that whole experience!

My time in Oxford drew to a close, and I packed up all my belongings once more. This time, I was free to find my own accommodation and I took time with the help of my younger brother and Sue to look for the right place where I could finally put down roots. One of the few

---

[30] Laurie Beth Jones, *The Path: Creating Your Mission Statement for Work and for Life* (New York: Hyperion, 1996).

requirements I was hoping for was to have a garden I could enjoy cultivating and which would be my therapy after busy and demanding days at work. God was incredibly generous in helping me to quickly find the perfect place.

11
Hospice Chaplaincy

Before I moved to Nuneaton, I went on a themed spiritual retreat based at Penhurst Centre, situated near to Battle, East Sussex. The topic of the week focused around the subject of New Beginnings and was very appropriate with starting out on a fresh chapter of my life. It was a well-timed week away and I sensed the retreat centre would become my favourite venue for future periods of time out. I was very comfortable with the size, the atmosphere of the house and the beautiful surrounding countryside.

As I spent time praying about the new venture in Nuneaton throughout the week's retreat, I penned the following prayer:

> Lord Jesus, as I move to Nuneaton and into a new ministry, would You please be in the centre of all I do and say. Please fill me with Your joy, laughter, intimate love and deep peace. Teach me to dance the dance You have for me, the dance which You know will touch those places of darkness within me where no one else will ever reach or touch. Create within me, please, Lord, the desire to seek Your face; create an imaginative spirit within me. Set me

alive, set me alight and set me free to be Your daughter.

On joining the hospice in 2011, I prioritised attending either an IGR or a themed retreat each year and it became an ongoing essential support mechanism for me. The combination of walking with people as they were approaching their end of life and supporting individuals after a loved one had died was incredibly intense. To be effective in both those areas I often found myself in what I would describe as a 'thin place' around the whole subject of death. People needed to know that I was willing to go to that place with them in our conversations and would sense if I were to draw back from such an emotional engagement.

I took time to read several books about end-of-life care and the issues around bereavement, and greatly valued a series of books written by Tom Gordon, who had been a hospice chaplain in Edinburgh. His first publication, *A Need for Living*, became my handbook as I considered it to be one of the most creative and honest accounts of hospice work, and I heartily recommend people getting hold of a copy. Tom is described as a 'soul watcher' by one of his students, which correlates with my expression of a 'thin place'. Tom states, 'I'm happy with that, because the desert, the companionship, sharing the tears, helping people move between their two rooms[31] are all about

---

[31] The two rooms equate to the process the person who is coming to the end of their life goes through as they journey closer to death but may still convey a few words or expressions to their loved ones.

watching the soul, entering into the life and struggles of the person for whom you would seek to care.'[32]

The gift of restoration

Taking quality space for an annual retreat to recoup from all I was absorbing was essential and healthy. It also enabled God to continue His work of bringing a much deeper layer of restoration into the inner parts of my life. We are all encouraged to pursue different stages of renewal, outwardly and inwardly, though always with the aid of the Holy Spirit. If we attempt to change personal negative habits in our own strength, our good intentions will invariably fail. The outward stages of restoration are much easier to see and grasp hold of – where we are seeking God to help us in changing unhealthy behaviour patterns.

We have probably all heard of people testifying to immediate changes as they have come to faith. God is in the lifelong business of transformation, and this endowment to His children is beyond measurement. The gift is readily available at any point in our lives, but God does not and never will force Himself on us. God always waits to be invited; He will initiate many opportunities for His children to accept and respond to, as we can read in the Song of Songs where a number of times He says, 'come with me' (eg 2:10b,13b; 4:8a).

---

[32] Tom Gordon, *A Need for Living: Signposts on the Journey of Life and Beyond* (Glasgow: Wild Goose Publications, 2001; reprinted 2007), p207. Used with permission www.ionabooks.com.

I have greatly valued this ongoing gift of healing and restoration and know how profound the process has been. Out of the broken, battered and damaged child, an ongoing healed, restored, beautiful child of God began to emerge. I am reminded of the incredible verse in Paul's letter to the Corinthians:

> 'My grace is sufficient for you, for my power is made perfect in weakness.' Therefore I will boast all the more gladly about my weaknesses, so that Christ's power may rest on me.
> (2 Corinthians 12:9)

God also understands there will be times when we may not be able to meet with Him intimately, that it feels too scary and too painful. Thankfully, He is more than capable of working with that level of honesty from His children. I have been encouraged by the verses, again in the Song of Songs, when the offer of an intimate encounter with God was turned down by the recipient (Song of Songs 5:1-3), as I know I have been in that position. Being utterly candid with God can bring about transformations as we face that heart cry and struggle within us. We yearn to draw close to Him, but it evokes deep pain as we attempt to trust Him. God is adept and willing to transform those areas deep within us that we want to change but, humanly speaking, it feels impossible to.

As we take time to look at other biblical passages on the themes of renewal, restoration and redemption, we can read how Jesus asks a blind man, Bartimaeus, 'What do you want me to do for you?' (Mark 10:51). Jesus didn't assume, take over, or put words into Bartimaeus' mouth.

It was essential that Bartimaeus spoke out his need and heartfelt request to be healed of his blindness. Likewise, we are given a similar courtesy when Jesus asks us the same question, 'What do you want me to do for you?' I wonder how we would reply right now to that request? It is a loaded question but so often can be given little consideration, maybe because of fear, or maybe out of a sense of low self-esteem. We can quickly dismiss the offer by thinking, 'I don't really matter; my needs are not as great as others'.'

Would we pass the offer by? Would we believe Jesus is interested enough in us individually to trust Him with our deepest needs and requests? On one of my retreats I wrote down without any hesitation what I wanted from Jesus:

> I want to be with You, to drink from Your well of living water. I desire to stay in the place of intimacy as Your child and not just during the times I am on a retreat. I want to fully embrace the ministry I feel God has called me to – in all its awe and humbleness. I want to radiate God's hope in the face of death and sorrow because without Him, I am nothing, and that is dangerous.

The gift of life

As I consider those requests I placed before Jesus and look at them afresh while writing this book, I know He has been incredibly faithful in answering them. One example where I know He has brought about immense personal change surrounds the whole concept of living life joyfully. For most of my adult life I would quite happily have seen my existence shortened. That doesn't mean I contemplated suicide, but life felt hollow, meaningless and monotonous. God's gift of restoration has thankfully amended those feelings.

I attended another themed retreat at Launde Abbey in Leicester during one Easter break, which was very special. The theme focused on the transformation process of a caterpillar changing into a butterfly, and understandably incorporated the Easter story. I realised how I had spent so long in the place of 'Good Friday', owing to all the pain and loss of my childhood. I recognised how often I had been stuck in 'Easter Saturday', where the caterpillar is being transfigured into the butterfly, but that metamorphosis hadn't quite happened. I could see the parallels in my own life where I had never quite believed the traumas of my childhood could ever be fully transformed, hence I had never fully grasped all the joys and celebration of 'Easter Sunday'.

I sensed my heavenly Father wanted me to surrender my ambivalence around death, to relinquish all the childhood pain inflicted upon me, to discard the fears of living and to hand over to Him those layers of mistrust. This is echoed in one of the psalms: 'For you, LORD, have delivered me from death, my eyes from tears, my feet from stumbling, that I may walk before the LORD in the land of the living' (Psalm 116:8-9).

I asked Jesus a slightly unusual question during some time out on the retreat: 'What do you want with me, Son of God?' His reply was awesome:

> I want you to stand alongside Me, being My precious child, My precious daughter, standing tall,

being My ambassador, My servant offering hope to all those who come your way. Being satisfied daily in all you face, realising the potential as you are and knowing there's even more ahead.

He also spent time with me addressing the concerns I had about being so alone during my childhood. I recognised how the cumulative impact of that deep sense of isolation had left me feeling empty, small, abandoned, cold and nameless. I took those painful emotions to the foot of the cross, knowing as I did so that Jesus' death and resurrection signified He had paid the price for my redemption. I sensed God say:

You, child, are filled with My love, you belong to Me. Your name, Gilana, has been chosen by Me. Drink in all that I offer you, child; drink deeply, breathe in My unconditional love, be held by Me. I will never let you go. Rest in Me, all that you need is right here.

God invites all His children to drink daily from His well of living water which refreshes, restores, renews and anoints. There we find incredible gifts of transformation, of healing and of connection.

In the past few years, I have become aware of an amazing story about the art of kintsugi which is said to have begun in the fifteenth century in Japan. It evolved from an accident where a precious tea bowl was broken and the subsequent repair to it was deemed inadequate. Further research into a better method of restoring the bowl brought about the art of kintsugi. The broken pieces of the bowl were repaired with gold dust, which still showed the original cracks, but the bowl could be put to use once more. Several Christian organisations are now using this concept to portray how God is well able to bring inner healing to those cracks in our lives.

Kintsugi Hope is one such example, established by Diane and Patrick Regan as a charity in 2017. Training groups have been established throughout the country aimed at making a difference to people's mental well-being. On his website, Patrick explains how we 'can discover treasure in our scars'.[33]

Without doubt, God has transformed and continues to renovate my horrendous scars into golden treasures. I used to hide from my scars and disown them, seeing myself as flawed and fearful, but I am God's masterpiece. I need to continually lift my eyes to Him and see myself as He sees me. We all need to remember how love and fear are opposites: God's love is freedom, human fear is imprisonment; God's love is spontaneous, human fear is crippling. As a result, I am now more spontaneous and accepting of the more vulnerable sides of me. Instead of the shame and exposure I had been subjected to, God continually demonstrates how He honours me with dignity, delight and splendour. Outstanding contrasts!

I began to feel for the first time in my life that I could 'sit back, let go and just be'. I started to experience the enjoyment of being like a child filled with wonder. I sensed I was losing the feeling of being 'haunted' and the 'I must keep going, or...' To be able to enjoy what may seem humdrum normality to many people means so much more to me. One of the best examples of this was walking

---

[33] www.kintsugihope.com (accessed 19th January 2020).

in the woods with Sue one autumn day. I stood in childlike wonder listening to the sound of the leaves swishing in the wind and watching them fall to the ground. We then spent time trampling through the leaves, giggling like two children! It was pure delight.

I joined the Mary Ann Evans Hospice in April 2011 with a dual role as hospice chaplain and head of the bereavement service (which was later changed to director of family services). I smiled to myself at returning to Nuneaton where I had become a Christian more than thirty years before at Lindley Lodge! Uniquely, the hospice in Nuneaton does not have an inpatient unit which, as time has gone by, has proved to be a wise decision. Hospices across the country have struggled to find the necessary funding each year to remain sustainable, especially in times of financial crisis.

My role as chaplain was incredibly varied, which I thrived on. I carried out my ministry in an informal style and firmly believed I needed to earn people's trust and respect over time. I only wore my dog collar on formal occasions as I recognised it could create a barrier of fear. The day unit was open Monday to Friday and could take up to fifteen patients at a time. It was not possible to link up with every person who attended, so that meant I needed to prioritise. I felt it was essential to spend time with those who were sadly approaching their end of life. I gently came alongside individuals and sought their permission to offer spiritual care to them, and to members of their family as well if necessary.

Quite early on in my time at the hospice, I was asked to talk at a community event: 'What does a hospice need from its chaplain?' I focused on the following strands: a chaplain has a consistent heart's desire of wanting the best for all; is willing to offer a helping hand; is wishing to walk alongside those who are in need; is praying to use all of their senses to go deeper with people as and when; is in tune with those times when it is essential to be quiet; is someone who knows their limitations; can smile, has a sense of humour and is able to think outside the box; and, above all, the hospice needs its chaplain to be a person of prayer in all that they do and say.

I dislike using jargon words and wish there was an alternative to the term 'spiritual care'. This can automatically provoke a barrier for many people who think they are going to be got at by the 'God squad'! When I asked people what their immediate reaction was on hearing the word 'spiritual', the vast majority replied that they linked it to religion. Spirituality is very difficult to define; as soon as you try to create a clear definition something is immediately lost, ie the mystery! Spirituality is about people and, as every person is different, the key to providing spiritual care is to understand what spirituality means for each person cared for under the umbrella of the hospice.

During a patient's journey of dealing with illness or impending death, their most significant and immediate spiritual need changes with time, according to their circumstances, mood and level of awareness of their prognosis. It was paramount to ask the patient or the person/people looking after their loved one what was most important to them in the here and now. When delivering holistic care, we need to remember there will always be concerns that we cannot fix. When we care for others, there will be tensions that we cannot relieve, some needs will go unmet and regrettably there may not be a soothing balm for the physical, emotional, spiritual or mental pain that people are dealing with.

Spiritual care is not about patching up broken lives or sticking a plaster over a wound. Spiritual care involves empowering others to live with, and through, anxiety and distress in a manner that feels right for them. If we can stay with patients' helplessness in difficult, irresolvable situations, we may truly be a comforting, hopeful and memorable presence. Saying 'I don't know' and still being available is spiritual care at its best.

Faced with cancer or any other serious illness, most of us may want to ask some deep questions: 'Who am I?' 'Why me?' 'What have I done to deserve this?' Often those questions are not raised with close family members, so it is essential to have the right person to turn to and to be brutally honest with. It is essential for hospice staff to form close relationships with those who attend the unit so that a level of trust can form and honest conversations can occur. If staff only stay on the surface in their conversations, permission is not being given for more in-depth talk.

It was always an amazing privilege to get to know the people who attended the hospice and to see how they changed over the ensuing months. So many came along feeling fearful and uncertain about whether they wanted to be there, but in time they were able to confidently 'own the building'. There is still a huge dread factor around attending a hospice, with the myth that they must be very depressing places. The apprehensions are intensified for those being admitted into an inpatient unit, as people worry that signifies the end of their life; they are going to die there. Both myths are so untrue!

There were always characters who stood out during their time at the hospice. However, it was important not to assume that there were no concerns hiding beneath their bravado. One such person was Fred,[34] who would go walkabout around the hospice, donating money each week to the fundraising team's raffle, chatting up the different receptionists and causing mayhem in the kitchen by ticking every item on the luncheon menu. He was most disappointed when he wasn't given the fundraising manager's job when it became vacant! He would often end up in my office to either attempt to wind me up or to talk more seriously as and when needed. I learned to recognise the clues when he wanted me to suggest a walk around the garden, which of course he would complain about, but he never refused the offer.

I spent many hours talking to his family before and after his death, and it was a great honour to take his funeral. This was one family where I saw the holistic 'joining up the dots' come to full fruition. Having a relationship with Fred led on to supporting the wider family, which in turn encouraged them to attend the annual Light up a Life[35] event at the hospice. It also enabled Fred's young grandson to attend one of the children's bereavement support groups and the monthly

---

[34] Not his real name.
[35] Light up a Life is an annual hospice event held in December whereby anyone can come and be part of a remembrance service.

drumming get-together, which gave Fred's daughter the opportunity to chat to other parents.

I designed a basic Spiritual Assessment form (see Appendix A) which was used to tease out important issues that patients might want an opportunity to explore. The questionnaire proved to be a useful tool on several levels; it was split up into four areas: family and friends, planning ahead, character and religious. One of the most important questions to ask is based around relationships. Making assumptions about people's liaisons is never a wise idea! The times I thought there would be no concerns when I sat down with someone, and I would be proved incorrect! If there have been breakdowns or there are frictions within the family unit, it is vital to give people opportunities to enable a reconciliation before it is too late.

Checking whether people had made a will and whether it needed updating, and if they had discussed their wishes with their family about the kind of funeral they would like were always imperative topics. People tended to fall into one of three camps concerning funerals: some said their loved ones wouldn't discuss it with them, but they were keen to get it arranged, others said the total opposite, and others had already organised their service. Funeral services are much more personal these days in terms of the choices of music and what is said. Where possible, it is ideal to work this through while the person facing their end of life has the energy to think about what they would like.

A dear lady I had known for some years and had enjoyed working with when she volunteered at the hospice was diagnosed with a terminal brain tumour. I met with her over the months following her diagnosis, as she wanted to plan her funeral and had asked if I would take it. I enquired if she wanted to write something to be included in the eulogy for her family as a parting gift to them. Her eyes lit up at this prospect and she thoroughly enjoyed writing some very special words to each member of the family. Sharing her thoughts at the funeral was incredibly poignant.

Because the hospice was a day unit, I was careful not to take over the role of a church leader for those people who professed to having a faith. My remit was to listen, and if I felt it was necessary to liaise with the person's church leader, I gained their permission to do so.

I was part of the multidisciplinary team, which involved weekly meetings to discuss all the people who came on board for some respite within the day unit. The team consisted of representatives from the nursing staff, the health care assistants, the complementary therapy staff, the bereavement team and, when necessary, a member of the lymphoedema group. I often found that patients would tell me information that the nursing team may not have been privy to, and it was essential for this to be disclosed and documented. The patients had given consent for their information to be shared across all the different departments with regard to their well-being at their initial assessment.

I was asked to see people if they were struggling with low mood or suicidal thoughts. Often people needed to be given permission to say they had had enough of living, but it didn't mean they were intending to end their lives. It was important not to panic or overreact during these occasions, but to gently unpack the statements individuals sometimes threw out. People who were coming to terms with a terminal diagnosis often kept their innermost thoughts and anxieties to themselves for fear of upsetting their loved ones. Attending a hospice allowed them to share these more difficult emotions if they wished to, and they were given the opportunity. My responsibility during these times was to listen, not to try to rescue, not to try to put a plaster over their wound (impossible to even try), as I mentioned earlier, and not to close the person down or to come out with glib statements! Staying with the individual in that place of uncertainty, allowing them to express fear or anger or worries for the people they were leaving behind was essential.

I would always check on people's general health – were they in pain, were they feeling sick, were they able to sleep, etc – as I often found they would reveal different information to me as a non-medic. I remember one lady who had a strong Catholic faith who shared with me how she was not taking her painkillers. As I gently pursued this conversation further, she revealed how she feared her priest would think she was contemplating euthanasia if she took her tablets.

By spending time with this lady, I was able to reassure her that the priest would not be considering such a thought. I encouraged her to have a conversation with him, which she did, and thankfully she started to take her medication regularly and her pain became more manageable.

I visited people in their own homes who were too poorly to come to the hospice, at the request of either the Hospice at Home team, one of the Macmillan nurses or the palliative care consultant. These requests needed to be carried out as quickly as possible and it was important to be quite direct (as well as showing a great degree of gentleness and sensitivity) with the person who wanted to see a chaplain. I never knew if I would have several visits or just one, owing to their deteriorating health.

Lengthy visits were out of the question as people tired quickly, and I was always aware that many other professionals may also be visiting on the same day. Families have often shared with me how they felt their homes were, without warning, invaded by so many professionals, from a GP (or locum), palliative care consultant, district nurse, Macmillan nurse, social services, Hospice at Home staff – and then add me! Despite these understandable limitations, those encounters were often very precious as people did not hold back in sharing their concerns, fears or questions. As time went on, and I gained more and more experience, I recognised that the most important factor for people to hold on to as they were approaching their end of life was based around love and relationships. Nothing else made sense in those final days.

I felt privileged to take funerals for the people I had worked with, but it was at times at a high cost to myself, as I became very close to some of those lovely ladies and gentlemen. I needed to maintain a high level of professionalism during those events, but it was then important for me to offload to a few others. My amazing chief executive, who was also my line manager, would always be willing to drive me to a difficult funeral, especially if it was at an unfamiliar venue, and be there to give me a hug afterwards, which was quite something as she was 'not a hug kind of person'! Emotionally I would be exhausted by large funerals, so asking someone to drive was important as my concentration levels were diminished after the service had finished.

There were several occasions when I was asked to put together a service for couples who wanted to renew their wedding vows, which was very special. I was responsible for organising the hospice's annual outdoor Light up a Life service where people were invited to come and remember a loved one who was no longer with them. I suggested a few years into my role that we needed to take this service into the different communities the hospice was involved in, rather than expecting everyone to travel to us.

It was always essential to gauge how much people wanted to know about their impending death or, if they were in their final few days of living, how much their loved ones wanted to know. Rightly, the emphasis these days is to allow people to die in their own homes if they wish to. As right as this is, family members looking after their loved ones in the final stages of dying may not be prepared for the physical deterioration. Watching a loved one die a difficult death is traumatic, especially if they are on their own at three o'clock in the morning.

I will always encourage both the person who is dying and family members to share anything they want to say before it is too late. Expressing our love, if appropriate, is essential even for the most reserved. If people become distressed or agitated during the last few days, it often helps to talk about good memories, or to look at a few favourite family photographs.

People have confided in me how they feel consumed by guilt for not physically being in the room when their loved one has died. The fact that they may have literally only gone out of the room for a few minutes to go to the bathroom or to answer the doorbell seems irrelevant to them. Again, I have heard so many times how some people who are dying wait until their loved one is not in the room before they die. Equally I have heard how some people who are dying wait until a member of the family who has had to travel some distance to see them arrives, and then they die.

I had pastoral oversight for all the volunteers and staff across the hospice and the shops. I would tend to go walkabout each day and gained a sense of when people wanted to chat. People knew that if my office door was open, they were always welcome to come and talk. A considerable part of my chaplaincy role involved offering reflective supervision to volunteers, bereavement and clinical staff. I often used coaching techniques as a helpful tool within those supervision sessions to inspire people to take personal responsibility for their own well-being. Using open-ended questions like what, how, when, who, where and tell me more meant I was not controlling those encounters but giving permission for individuals to own the process. My responsibility was to create a safe and confidential space, to listen deeply, to reflect back and not to fix the situation.

Five months into my new role at the hospice, my older sister, who had been battling with cancer, died. After her initial treatment she had enjoyed some years of remission, but the cancer returned, this time to her liver and lung before spreading to her spine and brain. I decided I wanted to take my sister's funeral for the sake of her two children; I didn't want someone they were unfamiliar with taking their mum's service. It was very special carrying out the funeral visit with my sisrter's husband and children over a buffet lunch with lots of memories, laughter and tears being shared. The children (both young adults) had specifically created pieces of music which they wanted in the service, and there were various poems her husband wanted to include.

I didn't regret my decision to take the funeral, but it was a highly charged, emotional and demanding experience. Thankfully, my younger brother drove me to the crematorium, which I hadn't been to before, but I almost lost my composure and ability to take the service when so many people came up to me beforehand expressing their sympathy. In the end I had to physically withdraw from everyone to regain a level of professionalism.

It took a good year to settle into my job at the hospice and to find a new spiritual director. By that stage I was aware that the feelings of not belonging were lurking around again and I sensed I was in a spiritual desert place. I had not found a suitable church where I could worship and be comfortable in; it was proving difficult to go anywhere local as so many patients and volunteers attended them, and I needed to be anonymous. Quite often by the weekends I was punch-drunk with intense conversations and needed quietness and space to recoup.

I also knew I needed to let go of the layer of cynicism and hurt as a result of my encounter with the curacy system. I needed to step away from the tunnel of my curacy experience! I sensed God draw close to me with His healing touch, which reassured me that I am loved and cherished by Him. It was important to lay before Him all the different emotions I had buried during the years of curacy and to seek Him afresh.

One of the dangers of working on the fringe of ministry is being viewed as a maverick; it was therefore vital that I always made myself accountable to a few key individuals, and my spiritual director was one of those people. Sessions with her tended to follow a pattern of spending the first fifteen minutes sharing how the past six weeks had been, then I was given a reflection relating to either some biblical verses or a section from a Christian book for me to sit with, pray and reflect on over the next half hour on my own. My director would then return to the room and I shared my thought processes with her. I was very aware she would have spent time praying before we met concerning what meditation to give me. Those meetings were always precious, provoking and powerful encounters with God.

It was so good to reach a place of contentment with the pattern of busy weeks alongside weekends of garden, space, reflective reading and peace. I knew I was in the right place serving God in Nuneaton.

I felt honoured to be invited to the twentieth anniversary of women's ordination, which was held in Coventry Cathedral in May 2014. During the service I recognised the phenomenal change God had initiated in me over the years. I was now at a place where God was encouraging me to 'fly' and to gently walk with the authority He had given me to minister and serve in His name, and to offer His hope and comfort to all those who were grieving.

I would often get asked what my job consisted of, which was almost impossible to say, as every day was so different. The main strands of my role involved managing a team of three staff and seventy-five volunteers;

interviewing and training staff, volunteers and students who wanted to undergo a bereavement placement; promoting the hospice through talks and training; being part of the senior management team; planning ahead suitable levels of expansion and monitoring the ongoing sustainability of the service; taking funerals; managing an 'I Matter' forum;[36] assisting in running children's groups; auditing and managing the bereavement's Excel database; designing appropriate questionnaires and leaflets; offering reflective supervision for all clinical nursing staff and the evening bereavement volunteers; undertaking one-to-one client support work; attending regular board meetings; managing the yearly budget for the bereavement service, applying for and managing specific grants of money; offering appropriate chaplaincy support to staff, volunteers, patients and their families; assessing all clients who requested support and matching them with the right volunteer or group.

My role as chaplain at the hospice was incredibly diverse and, even though it may sound strange to say, it was deeply rewarding. I felt humbled and privileged to be part of people's final journey on earth. I always ensured prayer was at the centre of all my daily activities, which was essential. I was also grateful for the faithful group of people who, over many years, regularly prayed for the hospice.

---

[36] More on 'I Matter' in the next chapter.

12
'I Matter'

In the latter years of my time at the hospice I attended another week's themed retreat which was based on transition and change. In the months leading up to and while on the retreat, I discerned God giving me a new initiative based around the words 'I Matter'. I clearly recall that in one of the evening meetings I became very focused on this process, and during some time out when we were encouraged to go and be creative, I mapped out all the thoughts that were going around in my head. I asked one of the leaders to join me so I could discuss with her all my thoughts and we spent time together exploring the concept and praying together.

The idea was to help people who were living with terminal illness to hold on to those amazing words, that they mattered. So often when terminal illness hits someone, bit by bit their lives can be taken over by medical appointments of one kind or another. There can be the inevitable chasing–up of medication or benefits, which can be time-consuming and debilitating. Then there is the whole process of treatment and the possible side effects to contend with. It can be so easy for the person's individuality to be swallowed up. You can undoubtedly feel like you are 'just a number' on an NHS computer.

When parts of us get 'stripped away', there is a danger of feeling that 'I don't actually matter'. We may feel a burden to our loved ones, we may feel we are being a nuisance to the medical profession and we can start to close down emotionally. Holding on to the valuable inner parts of who we are is essential, hence the concept of 'I Matter'.

As I returned home and continued to pray and think through this new concept, I read an article written in the *Church Times* by Ann Fulton, the spiritual care coordinator based at St Margaret's Hospice in Somerset. The article, entitled 'Caring for Each Person as a Spiritual Being',[37] excited me as it was echoing some of the thoughts I was working through. I had shared my ideas with a senior clinical colleague who was equally excited, so we decided to go to visit the hospice to meet with Ann to hear first-hand about her own initiative. Even though it was a long day, we made full use of the lengthy train journeys there and back to bat our ideas around – how we wanted to incorporate the 'I Matter' model into our hospice.

What I hadn't realised is that the phrase 'I Matter' is identical to one of the key mantras Dame Cicely Saunders, the founder of the modern hospice movement, had at the centre of her pioneering work. Dame Cicely was one of the key influential people in opening St Christopher's Hospice in 1967 in Sydenham, London.[38]

We decided it was important to roll out the 'I Matter' initiative to hospice staff and volunteers first of all, to encourage them that they counted, individually. If staff and volunteers didn't feel they were important, then how

---

[37] *Church Times*, 6th January 2017.
[38] www.stchristophers.org.uk (accessed 18th April 2020).

could we expect them to engage fully in this valuable belief we wanted patients to take hold of? Once we had spent quality time with the staff and then our team of volunteers, we would work with our patients.

I had grasped that people who were born and had lived their entire lives in Nuneaton sometimes struggled with feeling that they were 'good enough'. This was certainly the case with some of the staff working at the hospice. It didn't help having a much larger inpatient hospice not so far away geographically. I wanted staff and volunteers to feel they were not the 'poor second cousin', but that they were significant and could shine in the work they were doing with the patients.

I devised a lengthy 'I Matter' framework questionnaire which I took to the Senior Management team for their agreement (see Appendix B). There was a fundamental consensus that for this concept to work, there had to be utter confidentiality. I would be asking staff to be candid in their feedback to me and they needed to know I could be trusted to honour their honesty. I was aware I was putting my own reputation on the line, which I was very happy to do, in order to encourage staff to see how valued they were in my eyes.

The questionnaire was split into two sections. The first section aimed to create a personal 'I Matter' working framework for everyone to keep hold of. Staff were asked to sign this part of the document and to keep a copy for themselves. The second copy would go into their personnel records to assist them and their line manager at their annual appraisals. The second section was aimed at trying to encourage individual departments to take more responsibility for solving problems when they arose. At the end of this section were two important questions about the myths that the hospice had to continually deal with. Every organisation has history, which can be a positive influence, but equally it can hold people back from moving forward.

Once staff had filled in the questionnaire, I met with each department to go through their responses. Again, I highlighted at each meeting that what they shared with me would remain confidential. All feedback from the questionnaires would be compiled into one document with no names attached. As you can imagine, this was a lengthy process but a hugely important one. I ensured the shop staff were given the same opportunity to be involved in the exercise, and the senior management team (including myself) was the last group of people to fill in the forms.

After I had met with every team, I processed all their replies into a report which went to the senior management team to digest and to see where changes needed to be made. One of the immediate results was to set up an 'I Matter' forum which met every six weeks, which I chaired. A representative from each department was expected to attend and to feed back the outcome of the meetings to their team. This was to ensure a much clearer communication channel. If a department didn't attend, they couldn't complain about not being involved or communicated to! It certainly improved people's awareness of their need to take responsibility for problem-solving any concerns that arose, rather than constantly expecting more senior staff to sort the issues out for them.

I published a newsletter from the meetings to make sure an ongoing openness prevailed as well as ensuring improved communication continued. Volunteers were then asked to choose representatives to join the forum, again with the aim of improving communication and teamwork. To encourage a healthier group dynamic, I ensured staff sat next to a volunteer from their department so there wasn't an 'us and them' scenario in the room.

People fed back how much they had appreciated and valued this enterprise; there was a more positive feeling and ownership of the essential values they wanted to hold on to.

The gift of 'clothing'

Right at the beginning of the Bible, as God is creating the heavens and the earth, He says, 'Let us make mankind in our image, in our likeness' (Genesis 1:26). That verse alone clearly evidences how we all matter to God. The final gift I want to focus on is related to the gift of 'clothing', which may seem unusual, but I believe it is a fundamental inheritance God offers His people. There are so many passages in the Bible about how God attires His children to equip them for different aspects of their lives.

It's illuminating to read how, right at the very beginning of His relationship with humankind, God shows His unconditional love by clothing Adam and Eve. They have broken the one commandment He asked them to honour when they ate the fruit of the tree of the knowledge of good and evil. Their disobedience sets in motion devastating consequences and ultimately changes their relationship with God. Yet, despite their actions, He still provides for them (Genesis 3:21).

Other aspects of God dressing His children relate to our need to be equipped for difficult situations; our ongoing walk with Him; and, most importantly, how 'clothing' can be used by God for physical and emotional healing. We have the astounding passage in Ephesians where we are encouraged to put on God's armour especially when we face difficult periods in our Christian walk:

> Therefore put on the full armour of God, so that when the day of evil comes, you may be able to stand your ground, and after you have done everything, to stand. Stand firm then, with the belt of truth buckled round your waist, with the breastplate of righteousness in place, and with your feet fitted with the readiness that comes from the gospel of peace. In addition to all this, take up the shield of faith, with which you can extinguish all the flaming arrows of the evil one. Take the helmet of salvation and the sword of the Spirit, which is the word of God.
> (Ephesians 6:13-17)

There is something all-encompassing about physically imagining putting on each layer of the spiritual armour every day, in the same way we put on our outer clothes. A belt around our waist can help to hold items of clothes together, so the belt of truth offers us a spiritual solidity. As a breastplate covers vital organs, it makes sense that spiritually we are called to wear a breastplate of righteousness to protect our conscience and heart. Walking in shoes of peace gives strength and resilience. We hold in one hand a shield of faith to defend against doubt and fear. We wear a helmet to protect ourselves from injury when on a building site, on a bike or on a horse. It therefore fits that we put on a helmet of salvation, as our minds can so easily question our relationship with God, our calling or our gifts. In our other hand we are exhorted to hold the sword of the Spirit to speak out against attacks on our being.

In Paul's letter to the Colossians, we are reminded to 'clothe [ourselves] with compassion, kindness, humility, gentleness and patience' (Colossians 3:12). There are occasions in the New Testament when items of physical clothing were used to convey God's physical healing. The woman who had suffered from internal bleeding for many years touched the hem of Jesus' cloak as she reached out to Him among a crowd of people and was immediately healed (Luke 8:43-45). There is a remarkable verse in the Acts of the Apostles where we are told, 'God did extraordinary miracles through Paul, so that even handkerchiefs and aprons that had touched him were taken to those who were ill, and their illnesses were cured and the evil spirits left them' (Acts 19:11-12).

During some time out on a retreat I met up with my spiritual guide, who invited me to choose a postcard from a variety arrayed on a small table to indicate how I had been feeling in the weeks prior to the retreat. I chose two postcards: the first was of a woman trapped in her circumstances, cowed, fearful and wearing a drab outfit; the second was of a woman bowing down in awe to the Spirit (which is how I wanted to be). I recognised how I often approached my time with God with a sense of wearing 'beggars' clothes' and I wanted God to change that perspective within me. As I spent time on my own in the chapel later that same day, I discerned God bringing several fears to my mind concerning various near-death experiences I had endured during my childhood. While naming the fears before God, I visualised those 'beggars' clothes' being disposed of.

When I met up with my spiritual guide the following day, I shared the experience with her and she encouraged me to spend time meditating on other related Bible verses, including these precious words from Isaiah:

> I delight greatly in the LORD;
> my soul rejoices in my God.
> For he has clothed me with garments of salvation
> and arrayed me in a robe of his righteousness,
> as a bridegroom adorns his head like a priest,
> and as a bride adorns herself with her jewels.
> (Isaiah 61:10).

Since then I have often consciously started my day, in my mind, physically 'putting on' those royal clothes and allowing them to permeate my being. It has been so important to dress myself in these beautiful garments the Father has given me and not to allow the 'beggars' rags' space any longer.

13
A Ministry to the Bereaved
Part One

As time went on, my energy and attention became focused on the hospice's bereavement service, and I would go so far as to say that this became my main ministry. I shared earlier how I had sensed God saying to me that 'this is the glove [ie the glove of priesthood] I am giving you to put on and it will fit perfectly' during the vocations course I had attended. This statement finally came to total fruition as I embarked on establishing a holistic bereavement service.

When I joined the hospice, a small but dedicated team of five bereavement volunteers had been offering an ad hoc monthly group meeting and a telephone befriending support service since November 2004. They were supported by a part-time bereavement coordinator and then a full-time chaplain. One of my first tasks was to carry out an audit of this service to evaluate its effectiveness. While people generally appreciated the phone calls, it was evident we needed to expand our bereavement support service. Understanding the culture of the communities the hospice was involved in was my next learning curve. As I carried out some research I discovered that Nuneaton was one of the most deprived and poverty-stricken areas in the county. (In a 2015 governmental report, Nuneaton and Bedworth borough had the highest level of deprivation, children living in poverty and priority families in the county of Warwickshire.)[39] It was therefore important to offer suitable strands of support that local people would feel at ease with. For instance, we realised that formal counselling would not sit comfortably with the majority of people who were requesting support.

Each year I set out my priorities for the bereavement service with the agreement of my line manager. In the first year my aim was to devise a basic bereavement training course that all volunteers and staff could attend, interview and train new volunteers and design appropriate paperwork for each stage of the bereavement processes. I added another useful book to my library, *Talking with Bereaved People*, written by Dodie Graves,[40] which became my template in devising the training course.

I was slightly cheeky as I went about increasing the team of volunteers by purloining people who were working in other areas of the hospice (though they did thankfully continue helping out in their original places as well). My line manager attributed this to volunteers having had a 'chaplain-style' conversation! We never needed to advertise for volunteers; word of mouth often resulted in people contacting the service directly.

---

[39] https://apps.warwickshire.gov.uk/api/documents/WCCC-1014-256 (accessed 6th July 2020).
[40] Dodie Graves, *Talking With Bereaved People: An Approach for Structured and Sensitive Communication* (London: Jessica Kingsley Publishers, 2009).

In the early days I would frequently meet up with my line manager and we would take time out of our diaries for an extended lunchbreak at a local garden centre. As we ate, we brainstormed the next step forward in developing and managing a holistic bereavement service. I valued the freedom she gave me and her support, and she also enjoyed being given the opportunity to be part of the process.

This may sound very strange, but it was through the bereavement work that the creative side of me began to find a voice. We are probably all aware that the left side of our brain is responsible for controlling the right part of the body and majors on logic. The right side of the brain encourages creativity but can be thwarted by fear, not wanting to fail, paying attention to the inner critic and not giving space to dream big dreams. Giving space for creativity to flourish in me was an incredible, unexpected but totally fulfilling side effect of the inner healing and counselling I had undertaken.

I asked one of the staff from the hospice on the outskirts of Nottingham to be my mentor. She had allowed me to join her pastoral care course when I was a theological student (it is so amazing how God joins the dots up!) at St John's College. She agreed to my request and I would telephone her on a regular basis in those early formative years. I greatly valued her support.

Our initial expansion in 2012 consisted of offering bereavement support to adults after they had attended an assessment. They were then offered one of two strands of support. They could attend some one-to-one sessions or join a monthly social group, which we fondly called Jigsaw. We ensured people knew that we were not a counselling service but that we were offering a support network. The Jigsaw groups were held on a Tuesday afternoon and the only place big enough to facilitate this was the hospice lounge. Patients who would have been coming in were offered an alternative day.

The Jigsaw groups were small in numbers with a maximum of four bereaved people and two facilitiators who ensured everyone was given an opportunity to speak if they wished. Light refreshments were offered and the groups met for an hour and a half. There was more to the Jigsaw groups than outsiders first realised. On the surface, the Jigsaw events may have looked like a very gentle social gathering, and questions were raised as time went on as to how long people should be coming to them.

I was very aware in the early days that I was probably the only person who saw the full picture, as I knew many of the people before they came on board for bereavement support through my chaplaincy role, and I carried out the initial assessments. Without a shadow of a doubt, Jigsaw worked by the very nature of its simplicity and a sense of ownership by the people and volunteers who came along, without encouraging dependency. Because we offered a seamless process of support, people felt able to grieve in a safe manner and were processing things in their own way within the umbrella of Jigsaw. I was at times quite humbled by what people shared about how they used the Jigsaw events and how they helped them at a meaningful level. That doesn't mean we became complacent; we always needed to evaluate the different levels of service we offered.

People were given the opportunity to attend more than one level of support and could move on from one option to another. Each of the bereavement strands of support were evaluated with a questionnaire which people were asked to fill in once they were discharged from the service.

Within six months we were at saturation point with the Jigsaw tea parties and we needed to expand, as we had outgrown the space in the lounge and adjoining rooms. We decided to offer Jigsaw on the Monday evening and the Tuesday morning as well as the afternoon. The Monday evening Jigsaw would be aimed at siblings whose loved ones had unfortunately died and for those who couldn't get to a daytime event.

We found ourselves on a steep learning curve, and when I assumed something, I would thankfully realise my mistake quite quickly. Amendments were made without it affecting those coming along for help. I had assumed the Monday evening and the Tuesday morning would follow the same pattern as Tuesday afternoon, but that was not the case. There was a very different flavour to the evening Jigsaw groups and the Tuesday morning ones. Ideally, people preferred to attend the afternoon group, but as that was full they came along to the morning one. The evening groups were valued by people who worked during the day or had other commitments.

The bereavement service had one room in the hospice to offer individual support sessions, and as time went on I had to make my office available as there was no other place. A solution to our urgent need for space came out of the blue.

During 2012 the government offered hospices the opportunity to apply for a grant of money for new buildings and listed bereavement as one of their criteria. It was a unique offer and one we felt we had to apply for.

We were desperate for a new building as we had severe space restrictions; we were unable to expand any further, even though we knew there was a constant need for quality bereavement support. Because of our lack of space, we were not able to advertise our service and we could not offer out our facilities to any of the community support networks like churches, funeral directors or GP practices. We had compiled a comprehensive in-house bereavement training course for all staff and volunteers and knew we could offer this piece of work to a wider audience, but needed the space to accomplish this.

We never imagined for one minute we would be successful with our application, but we had nothing to lose. We were absolutely delighted, amazed and a little scared when we heard we had been granted a considerable sum of money. We were awarded a grant of £530,000 to build a new two-storey building overlooking the hospice gardens. This would allow the hospice to expand its present service, and the new building was scheduled to be ready for use by July 2014. The board of trustees agreed to free up hospice funds to cover the deficit.

At the beginning of 2013 I attended a supervision course in Oxford which confirmed the growing sense within me that we needed to review the service's expansion. I had no formal bereavement qualifications and therefore took time to visit other more experienced people in the bereavement field. This was vital on a few occasions when I sensed there were potential vulnerabilities in some of the foundations of our service as we began to expand.

The bereavement service was run almost on a shoestring; it was highly dependent on volunteers who in the main were excellent, but there was a constant need for good managing and steering. As quickly as we increased the number of volunteers to help with the different strands, we also lost some as they faced their own bereavement or health issues. There were times when we came close to running some of the Jigsaw groups without enough facilitators. I recognised that there would always be personnel issues which would need to be addressed and to ensure they didn't affect good practice.

Every time we looked to expand the service in those early years, we needed to check on the issue of sustainability, which was a tricky balancing act given the other part of my role as hospice chaplain. At any moment I had to know someone else could step into my bereavement shoes if my chaplaincy role needed to take precedence. Visiting very poorly patients, supporting their families and planning funerals always took priority. There was never any warning to these demands, so we always had to work with the unknown. The chief executive kindly stepped in for me on occasions with the monthly Jigsaw gatherings, but it was becoming trickier for her as her role was also expanding.

Despite the constraints of limited space in the hospice we still managed to offer other new levels of bereavement support, including a monthly 'Sanctuary' communion group for those who valued space to work through concerns they had regarding their faith, pre-bereavement support which was offered within my role as chaplain, and an opportunity to meet with the hospice's palliative care consultant for those who were struggling with some medical issues after the death of a loved one. This proved to be an immensely useful opportunity for people who felt they could not move forward in their grief while they struggled with medical questions or the treatment their loved one had gone through.

We could not ask more of our amazing volunteers; they already gave a huge amount of time, and the overall steering of the service needed additional paid members of staff at the helm. My workload was increasing all the time, and balancing both roles was becoming more intricate. The bereavement side of my role already took more than half my time, and with the extra demands of a new building ahead of us it would continue to do so.

I recognised that bereavement could become an unmanageable beast if not carefully handled. We had to take one step at a time in ensuring new volunteers were well trained; volunteers who had settled in were consistently offered supervision and encouraged. Any areas of expansion had to come under the remit of an inexperienced team who were learning the skills as they went along. Ethically, we needed to ensure we abided by the recommended safe practices.

There was always a danger of overreaching and expanding the service too quickly. There were very few experienced people involved, and I included myself in that. We were on steep learning curves not only personally, but also in evaluating and taking the service forward. There was a high emotional cost to the support we provided, and that had to be carefully managed to avoid burnout. There were only so many referral assessments I could undertake in any given week, and I constantly encountered raw grief and soaked up the many distressing experiences people had gone through.

My line manager witnessed that ongoing emotional impact on me and generously gave me time to offload. I would often go either into her office or to the fundraising team and demand chocolate after gruelling assessments!

I cannot emphasise enough how scary doing this work was at times; we were dealing with very vulnerable people and we were learning as we went along. I compiled a report detailing all these concerns for the board of trustees to consider how more funding could be made available for the bereavement work. Thankfully, they agreed more paid staff were needed and adverts went out to recruit two part-time members of staff.

We had about a year to prepare for the new building, and there was an acknowledgement of the importance of using this period to prepare for the next stage of expansion. The new build would help hugely in terms of space, but we needed wisdom in how and when to expand. It was essential we took appropriate time to prepare for the expansion into the new building.

We formed a group consisting of experienced bereavement volunteers, the chief executive, the head of operations and myself. We invited a representative from the hospital's bereavement centre to join us as well. (The hospice was situated on the same grounds as the hospital and we worked closely with them.) The group was fondly called the 'Potting Shed' and we split ourselves into three teams and were given different mandates. It made perfect sense to put a project together to offer a better model of support for the families our Hospice at Home staff were engaged with. We aimed to offer further training to six experienced volunteers who would work alongside the Hospice at Home team. They would link up with the team on an initial bereavement visit and then offer the necessary bereavement support while the nursing staff moved on to supporting other families.

An important element was to expand into the community, so we aimed to contact the funeral directors, the crematorium and the local churches to offer and advertise our services. It was possible that some churches would want us to offer them some training. We also aimed to contact all the GP practices in our locality to let them know about the bereavement support we were offering. We wanted to be very careful about this, bearing in mind we did not want to step on the hospital's bereavement service toes in their contacts with local GPs.

The Potting Shed group would look at how we expanded in house with drop-in sessions, reconfiguring the Jigsaw events, short-term workshops offering practical support, increased pre-bereavement support, new areas of training both in house and externally, joined-up work with the hospital, and talking to our present users on where they saw gaps in the strands of support. The group worked on compiling a mission statement for the bereavement service in readiness for our move into the new building: 'a place where there is permission to laugh; to cry; to hold back; to move forward; where there is freedom to be honest without feeling the need to protect others; and where clichés are not used to hide away from raw pain'.

The next phase in our planning was focused on designing a brochure to explain and promote our services with a covering letter to tweak accordingly concerning all the different strands listed above. We felt it was important to visit other bereavement centres where new builds had already happened, and to link up with the local colleges that offered counselling courses. The bereavement service had started to take on some counselling students from one college and we knew we could offer the same opportunities to other colleges seeking student placements. Students were required to see a certain number of clients, which gave them hands-on experience within a supportive environment as part of their training. In return we ensured they were well supervised and gave them further opportunities to gain experience in our other models of bereavement support, which they wouldn't have received elsewhere.

We needed to advertise, interview and train a considerable number of new volunteers. We wrote to thirty people who had received bereavement support from the hospice and were now in a better place emotionally. We asked them to join us as volunteers for the new building. All thirty people wanted to come on board, but a few were not able to at that time, owing to other commitments. Many of them staffed our new reception desk, which was such an important role. They all knew from personal experience how grief had affected their lives and how difficult some people found entering a building for the first time with raw grief etched on their faces.

As you can see, this was a huge undertaking on top of our ongoing workloads, but it was still exciting to be involved in! In all my working life I have never experienced the atmosphere that was present in the Potting Shed meetings; there were no egos in the room and we were all equal. There were huge joys in working with a fantastic team of volunteers (and the part-time staff who joined the service later). They all contributed to the bereavement service working creatively, sharing the vision and bringing their ideas, passion and commitment together.

14
A Ministry to the Bereaved
Part Two

Two years later the bereavement service moved into the amazing bespoke building adjoining the hospice, which we named the Warren. Why that name? Firstly, I had been working with a lady who was a long-term supporter of the hospice and had been one of the original five bereavement volunteers. Sadly, her husband, whose name was Warren, had died. As she walked out of my office one day, I felt using his name would add a suitable personal touch to the new building. We, of course, got her permission.

Secondly, when you think of a warren, you can conjure up the image of it being a warm, safe place; a refuge to turn to when needed. A warren also has many twisting tunnels going in all directions, which at times may feel dark and scary. This image can mirror the journey many people describe as they walk the path of bereavement. There can be a sense of going down different and confusing cul-de-sacs when grieving in the same way that a warren has different tunnels.

It was incredible how the building enveloped the hospice gardens in such a way that it looked like a large tree house! So many people asked if they could personally hire a room out for a week's holiday! We had three one-to-one rooms upstairs, two of which had their own balconies looking out on to the garden. The third was a larger room which we used with children on a one-to-one basis as it had a large bay window. Children of all shapes and sizes loved to clamber onto the bench seat and surround themselves with numerous teddy bears. The largest room was used for the Jigsaw social groups, training and general meetings. So much of the interior decorating of the rooms reminded me of the importance of having a therapeutic environment to enable healing, and the Warren rooms allowed this in bucketfuls.

The Warren building empowered the team to develop a caring, safe and confidential atmosphere for vulnerable, hurting people to receive gentle support. The Warren's mission statement really did give people permission to be themselves. We fully recognised that a few individuals would never get over their grief and needed the constant support and acceptance that was on offer from the service.

Many people who were grieving were less than gentle with themselves and needed encouragement to be patient and tolerant with themselves. If we allow grief to take its natural course we will emerge into a different place within ourselves. But the process needs patience and understanding. I often likened it to having a broken leg – you can see the physical manifestation of a leg in plaster and know how not to cause further damage or delay the natural healing. When grief happens, our hearts are broken, but we cannot see the damage that has been inflicted on one of our most precious organs. A broken heart needs a great deal of tender care and gentle nurture in order for healing to occur.

Anyone could be referred to the service; they didn't have to have a previous connection with the hospice. There were many times I wondered how on earth we could continue to facilitate such a service as it grew every year by at least 20 per cent in terms of the number of referrals received. There was no pattern from month to month on how many people would request support, and we ensured people were not kept waiting for an assessment. With a great deal of underlying prayer, without fail, a volunteer was always found who was happy to take on another client.

The bereavement team grew to seventy-five volunteers and three part-time members of staff (excluding myself). Working with staff and volunteers in a team environment has strengthened my view of how important it is to value contributions, feedback and ideas from a diverse group of people. My role as the years went on was to steer this amazing 'ship' and to enable staff and volunteers to feel confident in their own abilities to support and walk alongside bereaved people. I constantly looked ahead to see where our next layer of expansion needed to be. I was also responsible for monitoring the ongoing sustainability of the service.

We were now offering more pre-bereavement support for families and for individuals who were sadly coming to the end of their lives. We started to provide support to people whose loved ones had tragically taken their own lives. With any new venture we would read appropriate literature and ask more experienced people for advice before embarking on it.

Many of our strands of support were initiated through conversations with people who came along for their assessment and shared what they were struggling with. That was certainly the case behind the reasons for designing our layer of support: Sanctuary. For some people, when grief hits, it can provoke a much deeper personal crisis as they tussle with various questions such as, 'What is life all about now that my loved one has died?' 'Is there meaning to my life any more?' 'Where is God in my grief?' Sanctuary was established and provided a quiet, reflective space which enabled people to process some of the above concerns.

We used our downstairs room in the Warren for this support mechanism. The gentle, calming environment of looking out on to the hospice garden added an important facet in allowing a healing element to the quiet space being offered. It was vital that we allowed people to work through their angst in their own way without any of the team 'interfering'. Silence is such an incredibly precious gift, which we ensured happened within the Sanctuary set-up.

Many people who attended Sanctuary hadn't set foot inside a church or may not have professed to having a faith, but were searching for deeper meaning and answers to life. Sanctuary honoured that process. It also allowed anonymity for people who were attending a local church but craved some quietness and permission to grieve in the way they needed. I watched broken people come along to those small, intimate groups and over time be gently mended. It was a humbling experience.

There were times when my dual role of chaplain and head of the bereavement service dovetailed. I have occasionally worked alongside individuals who hadn't been able to attend a funeral or were not allowed to be involved in planning a funeral service, which had left them highly distressed. I would work with them to put together a different kind of 'service', not to re-enact a funeral event, but an alternative one which would give that person a good memory. They would choose the content of this 'service' and we would read through it when they felt ready; it was again an incredible healing process.

I also offered spiritual accompaniment to a number of people who were grieving and struggling with difficult emotions around their relationship with God. Again, these folk needed anonymity and permission to express difficult faith concerns without being judged. These encounters were always deeply rewarding, and many times I would come away humbled at how honest and open people were at a time of difficult life experiences.

I shared the concept of creating a 'safe place', which I had personally found so spiritually therapeutic during my time at theological college, with my bereavement colleagues and a few of the more experienced volunteers. We started to use this model with people who had gone through traumatic grief experiences and felt they were trapped in distressing memories. We were incredibly careful with this model, initially spending time explaining the process and suggesting people took a while to think it through before their next support session. If they wanted to proceed, we provided large, blank sheets of paper, crayons, pens and paint and encouraged folks not to worry about their level of artistic skills.

Strong, clear boundaries were established; sessions would be a mixture of initially checking how the client was and encouraging them to create their own 'safe place' and to draw it on paper, explaining all the important elements that gave them a sense of security. This was not rushed as it was an essential foundation before moving on to the next stage. If people struggled to work out what their safe place was, we would gently give some examples others had used (without breaking confidentiality). Once they were satisfied with their 'safe place' we reminded them they could return to it at any stage if they felt too uncomfortable with the next part of the process. On a fresh piece of paper, we asked them to begin exploring the distressing emotions around their trauma by drawing images or writing words down as they came into their heads. We kept a close watch on the time as it was essential the client ended the session by going back to their safe place to ensure they left the session in an OK condition. The process proved to be deeply beneficial as people were able to look creatively at their experience in a different manner and to make astonishing shifts and changes.

The first time I suggested using this technique was with a lady I will call Sally whose husband's cancer had ravaged different parts of his body over several years. This roller-coaster nightmare was intensified by him going through episodes of losing consciousness, being hospitalised and Sally being warned by the medical team that he might not survive this latest crisis. The next day he would be sitting up in bed, demanding toast! When Sally referred herself for bereavement support after the death of her husband she was, in her own words, 'manically overdriven'. We spent some months talking through different elements of her grief and came to a stage where Sally felt overwhelmed by the many difficult memories.

Sally agreed to try the above technique and designed her safe place as a chalet on a beach, drawing in detail what furniture went in the chalet. On a fresh piece of flip chart paper Sally wrote down a vast array of words expressing all her pain, distress and frustration surrounding her husband's illness and death. She held nothing back; raw, honest words were written down and she linked all the words up by drawing barbed wire to signify the intense damage inflicted. We spent some sessions on this exercise, always ensuring Sally kept hold of her safe place. When Sally was ready, she took another piece of paper and wrote down all the good memories she had shared with her husband, and this time linked them all up by drawing hearts. It was a powerful contrast and helped Sally immensely.

Towards the latter part of 2014 we took a very deep breath and made the major decision to offer children and young people bereavement support now our new building was up and running. As an organisation we had always stressed that we supported the patient and their family, but that was only if they were over the age of eighteen, which couldn't be described as holistic!

We were successsful in applying for a grant of money from Children in Need[41] for this new piece of work and went into partnership with a local counselling organisation that was highly trained in working with children. They came and spent time training a group of volunteers and staff to work alongside children. They kindly joined in with the first few years of working with the youngsters, encouraging and advising us when

---

[41] www.bbcchildreninneed.co.uk (accessed 22nd May 2020).

necessary. I knew we were making the right decision in offering children support, but personally it was ringing some alarm bells inside me. I had already recognised how being involved in bereavement work continually touched an inner 'heart' core, which was absolutely as it needed to be; walking alongside people in that 'thin place' of death.

Taking that heart process to another layer by working with children and young people provoked huge fears within me. I wasn't sure if I could work with youngsters, given my own inner frailties, but I was determined to work through the reasons triggering my reactions. My personal fears could not get in the way of the hospice expanding its support network further. I contacted my spiritual director and saw her on a weekly basis for some in-depth counselling to help resolve those concerns. Thankfully, as I did this, the fears dissipated and I could freely embark on the next step and lead this valuable new stage of work.

We learned so much working with children and young people and it was a delight having them in the Warren building. Children handle grief so much more easily than adults, especially when they are given permission to express their different emotions. Too often adults understandably try to protect youngsters from the pain of grief and unwittingly can provoke anger if they haven't involved the young person in their loved one's deterioration and ultimate death. Young people can and do cope with terminal illness and death when they are given the space to talk in their own style about their loved ones.

In the main, children worked better in groups as they needed to meet others of the same age to realise they were not the only ones dealing with sadness. Their weekly get-togethers involved listening to an appropriate story, designing a memory box and bringing in special mementoes they wanted to put into their box to remember their loved one; they talked as they undertook different activities, such as creating a broken heart out of clay, making a worry monster and designing a memory jar. Once the children had completed their six- or eight-week programme, they were invited to return for a monthly follow-up drumming group as a support mechanism.

Youngsters aged thirteen and upwards preferred to receive one-to-one support, which we facilitated with appropriate creative exercises. More teenagers were being referred to the unit for pre-bereavement support and we encouraged them to work together in a group. It took a huge amount of organisation, finding enough volunteers and picking the right early evening of the week that everyone could attend. We therefore decided to offer half a dozen teenagers the opportunity of coming for a pre-bereavement programme on a Saturday. We were able to use the whole building and designed a roller-coaster theme throughout.

Whenever we work with youngsters we have to be prepared for the unexpected, and this was certainly the case with the group who attended on the Saturday. When they arrived, one of them found the prospect of being in a group too much and closed down emotionally before our eyes. Instinctively we knew we had to steer him very gently into a room upstairs, and two of us spent the day allowing him to gently come out of his shell. It was such a valuable lesson allowing this youngster to dictate the pace he wanted to work at during the day. We checked whether he wanted to go home or stay, and we ensured that he knew he could join the group at any point if he desired to, including during the lunchbreak.

He clearly wanted to play a number of games we had in our store cupboard in the morning, and Jenga became his favourite. We had adapted the game by writing different questions on the bricks, all related to bereavement, which we all had to answer when we pulled a brick away from the tower. By the afternoon he became more involved in the timetabled programme, which we adapted as we went along with him, as he still wanted to be on his own. As the day wore on it was heart-warming to watch him shine, and a very different young man literally bounced out of the room when it was time to go home.

The hospice received very little money for its bereavement work, so most years I would explore and obtain other avenues of income from grant organisations to enable the ongoing expansion of the service. The week before Christmas a few years ago my line manager discovered that a major charitable organisation was linking up with Hospice UK,[42] the national charity for hospice care in this country. A considerable sum of money was being offered for new bereavement projects that included strong community links as their main criteria. My line manager and I both knew we needed to put in an application, even though the deadline for submissions was less than a few weeks away.

After a few false starts I came up with the idea of a community initiative and partnership working with three

---

[42] www.hospiceuk.org (accessed 22nd May 2020).

local funeral directors and the crematorium to offer a drop-in session for newly bereaved people. We believed it was the first time such an initiative had been tried across hospices. I had the advantage of knowing the funeral directors and the staff at the crematorium through my chaplaincy work, so we already had good working relationships.

We called the initiative Stepping Stones, with the aim of people starting off in a drop-in group but being able to access our other strands of bereavement support as and when they wished. We also hoped to use this project to promote the bereavement service within the locality. Many people were still not aware that they could access support even if they hadn't had any hospice involvement. A third aim was to increase our referral rate by an extra sixty people (adults and children) over the year.

There was an overwhelming number of requests for the grant money across the whole of the United Kingdom. We were therefore flabbergasted and delighted to be the only day hospice and one of only nine hospices overall to be successful with an application.

The initiative was a huge undertaking as it involved recruiting and training a new team of volunteers and ensuring the project stayed within the budget of the grant of money received. We needed to design a series of questionnaires to evidence changes in people's lives through the support they received. It was important to spend time liasing and promoting the project with our community partners. We were required to attend several workshops in London with Hospice UK, who were overseeing the grant.

We also had to ensure our other strands of support remained sustainable at the same time. Thankfully, we were able to employ one of our fabulous volunteers, covered by the grant money, to help out with all the administrative tasks linked to the project.

It was a very different piece of work as we never knew who would turn up to a Stepping Stones session. We offered this specific support three times a month with one of the funeral directors hosting a drop-in session. That in itself was a new experience for our team – to take a bereavement session in an unfamiliar environment.

By now, you would have thought I had stopped making the mistake of assumptions! The afternoon when I said to my team, 'It's OK, we will have a quiet Stepping Stones session,' it turned out to be anything but! A family of five turned up, all needing individual support, and we quickly had to move other folk around to ensure they were given quality time and care. Our team of volunteers came along to every session knowing they may hear the immortal words from yours truly, 'Your mission for today is…' They knew this meant they were being asked to do something different from what they had come along expecting to do. It was to their incredible credit that they were always willing to think outside the box and to go with meeting the needs of the person who had just walked through the door.

As the year's project drew to a close, we were visited by two members of the Hospice UK team who wanted to hear first-hand how we had found the experience. We ensured they met a number of the volunteers who had been part of the project, our administrator and the two senior members of staff who had managed the Stepping

Stones sessions. We managed to achieve the targets we set with this project. Our relationships with the funeral directors and the team from the crematorium were strengthened. We were asked to share our newly designed questionnaires with other hospices. However, after the year's grant was used up, we decided not to continue with this strand of support. Stepping Stones had stretched our resources to an uncomfortable place, and we all agreed it had been a useful project but was unsustainable long term.

The two people from Hospice UK wrote a lovely complimentary email to the people they had met on their visit. They thanked everyone for sharing their thoughts about the project with them. They appreciated my feedback about the specific challenges I had faced around the extra evaluation methods needed to evidence the outcomes of the project on top of an incredibly busy workload. These challenges had been expressed by other smaller hospices who didn't have the advantage of employing extra staff who were experienced in audit and research methods. They were bowled over at the holistic strands of bereavement support on offer and how we were so dependent on volunteers.

I encountered one of the first people who had come along for some bereavement support through the Stepping Stones project in my local supermarket a short while ago. He had used the different layers of support as we had hoped, coming on board for the initial drop-in session, moving on to a Jigsaw social group and accessing a few one-to-one sessions. He was extremely grateful to all the people who had supported him.

I was interviewed by Hospice UK to coincide with the completion of the Stepping Stones project. I was asked what I was passionate about. I answered:

> I am passionate about walking alongside people in whatever they are going through. To offer compassion without being intrusive and to always display integrity. To draw people in from the fringes and to welcome those who are not immediately accepted by others. To take God into places where it is not the 'norm' and to avoid jargon words.

The second question was, if I could share three things about what excited me, what would they be? My reply was, 'All people matter to God, ask the impossible and let God do His stuff.'

It was always a joy to see someone work through their grief and come to a place where they then wanted to offer their time to the hospice as a bereavement volunteer. There were always openings for people to join the team, on the reception desk at the Warren, offering to make cups of tea, being willing to drive people to and from the building, helping out with the administration or being involved in one of the strands of support.

Working with bereavement can change you quite profoundly in a positive way. I recognised over the years how the gifts of compassion, empathy, listening deeply, wisdom in knowing when to say something or when to be quiet, a greater sensitivity and gentleness were generously provided for me by God. It also meant I needed to continually go deeper myself in my relationship with God in order to be His effective channel. As I wrote earlier, bereavement can be an unmanageable beast to handle if you are not careful. Regular time out to avoid burnout was essential.

If I was asked to sum up our holistic bereavement service, I would say, 'Believe the impossible can happen,' and, 'From tiny acorns mighty oaks have grown.'

15

Talking About Death and Honouring Death

Talking about death

Experiencing someone else's grief is not regarded as a comfortable emotion for those who have not undergone a loss themselves. People can become impatient with those whose loved ones have sadly died, when they don't feel they are recovering as quickly as they feel they should be and and cannot comprehend why they are not ready to 'get on with life'.

There seems to be a lack of understanding about the immense value of loving someone over a lifetime and the sheer depth of pain that is evoked when death occurs. The phrase, 'Are you feeling better now?' can be quickly bandied around and can come across as quite insensitive to the bereaved person. People struggling with grief are often supported for about three months and are then left to their own devices. I frequently used the image of a pair of weighing scales when talking to people who were newly bereaved and were feeling guilty about not being able to move on. If on one side of the weighing scales you put the amount of years you have loved someone – eg forty to fifty years – and then on the other you put the amount of months you have been grieving, you would quickly see the huge imbalance!

We unfortunately live in a society where people crave instant quick fixes, but grief cannot and should never fit into that context. Love is not a commodity to be dispensed with instantaneously. To the depth to which we have loved a person, so we will suffer the same depth of pain, loss and anguish.

The loss of a wife, a husband, a partner or a child has always elicited sympathy, but the loss of a mother, father, sister, brother or friend doesn't gain the same recognition. Those people are often left to get on with their grief silently, and understandably often feel quite alone.

Some people have spent ten or twenty years, or even a lifetime, looking after their loved one, so when they die they feel like they have lost their identity alongside suffering their grief. They have no idea how they are going to use the endless hours they suddenly find themselves with each day, each week, each month.

We are equally not great in this country about discussing death; culturally we seem to have gone backwards in having healthy discussions on this topic. In our parents' era it was not uncommon, when a death occurred, for the body to be in an open coffin in a side room at home for people to visit and pay their respects. Nowadays there seems to be so much fear around even discussing death; I would often say to people how talking about death wouldn't hasten our end of life!

To help people become more comfortable in talking about death, the bereavement service designed several training programmes. The very first one I compiled at the start of my time at the hospice was quite basic. I always tried to ensure our training courses were as interactive as possible. 'Talking at' people and seeing their eyes close is, as far as I am concerned, not conducive to great learning! We knew people would feel fearful and nervous about spending time looking at grief. At the end of a training session attendees often remarked on how much fun they had had, which they had not expected!

It was essential to cover the mandatory topics such as confidentiality, so we adapted the game of Cluedo to ensure people stayed engaged alongside understanding this important subject. Paddington Bear's story was a great hit, as staff and volunteers got to speak out various parts in their best theatrical manner! Paddington was the key player in unpacking spiritual, physical, psychological and social needs around every encounter with a patient.

Making use of salt-filled spice jars was a powerful tool in helping people share with each other about their own experiences of a loved one dying. We invited people to spread out the salt onto four small pieces of paper and place one mound of the salt onto a larger piece of paper. They were asked to choose a coloured chalk and then to share with the person next to them four good memories of their loved one as they coloured in each of the salt mounds with different coloured chalks. People went away with a coloured spice jar to remind them of precious memories. It is a known fact that some people need to be doing something with their hands to talk more freely, and this was evidenced with this exercise. We used a ball of wool, statements typed up on cards and some pegs to demonstrate the complexity of grief as the wool was thrown to people around the room in random, chaotic order. The team would always warn people that emotions may be evoked during the creative exercises and ensured a spare quiet room was free next to the training room.

We banned people from using any euphemisms while they were on one of our courses. I was surprised when I explored the different expressions people used as alternatives to saying someone had died. There were more than thirty phrases people frequently used, alongside some very odd ones! We have all heard people say their loved one has passed away, fallen asleep, departed, gone, slipped away, met their Maker or been lost. We also strongly discouraged any of our volunteers from using the phrase 'moving on'. There was a danger of people who were grieving feeling they were being judged and that they should have been in a different emotional place if they heard that phrase.

More in-depth training was offered to health professionals, initially focusing on the huge importance of listening. To listen well, we must be willing to 'dare to go there', to ask people how they are doing, to invite them to talk and share if they wish to. We need to be willing to stay with them in what may feel an uncomfortable conversation. Often, our own fears and discomfort stops us from going there, and those incredibly important conversations never happen. The training would then move on to looking at the fears and discomfort around death and dying. We asked people to look at the following questions on their own and, if they were comfortable, to share their answers within the group:

What are your personal experiences of someone dying / their death / your bereavement?

Are there family members with whom you have a difficult relationship?

What would you want to say to them, if you were dying?

What are your fears about your own death?

How would you prefer to die?

What do you find difficult talking to patients about?

What do you think happens when you die?

What are your fears about the deaths of those you love?

What emotions might you find difficult when talking to a patient?

The training team went on to give people two blank pieces of paper and asked them to write down four things they would like to happen if they were dying, and four things they would not like to happen.

My wonderful team of reception volunteers happily cut out cardboard jigsaw pieces for the next strand of training. On each jigsaw piece was a statement people coming to their end of life had shared with me over time, which were: honesty, enjoy today, say I am going to be OK, dignity/respect/privacy, don't take over my home, love, eat and drink, my decision, just 'be', express fears, say goodbye, listen, prepare, and why?

People got into pairs and their first challenge was to make a jigsaw with the pieces they had in front of them. Of course, there was no finished picture for them to use as a guideline! Two pieces of the puzzle had a statement on them that didn't fit, and I asked them to note which they were as they were making the jigsaw. They were given ten minutes to create their masterpiece. No one managed to complete the puzzle because I had fiendishly ensured that couldn't happen!

I questioned people as to why they thought I had given them a jigsaw that didn't fit together. I went on to explain how there were no perfect endings with palliative care!

I went back to the question about which two statements people felt didn't fit in the jigsaw. The answer was, 'say I am going to be OK' and 'eat and drink'. So many people shared with me as they were coming to their end of life how they did not appreciate the glib throwaway statements of, 'You are going to be OK,' either from medical professionals or from people who were not so close to them. Families equally shared how distressed they became by all their attempts to encourage their loved one to eat and drink. If only they had been given the advice that this wasn't an issue at all for their loved one and that not eating or drinking much at this stage would not hasten their death. What was far more important was for their loved ones to spend the quality time left with them.

There are lots of good intentions around palliative care, but sometimes we can try too hard with the wrong things. We can get caught up with the dynamics around the understandable need to respect people's wishes, but sometimes end up colluding with delusion. I gave people an example of a lady, who we called Mary, who came along to the day hospice and was very distressed. The nursing team asked me to see Mary, who told me her family didn't want her to tell their dad she was living with a terminal diagnosis of cancer. Her mum had Alzheimer's and the family felt it was too much for him to know about her condition on top of caring for his wife.

What would your first question be to Mary? The answer hopefully is, 'Mary, what do you want to happen?'

Over several weeks, Mary and I worked on whether she felt comfortable with her dad not knowing the truth about her condition, and how he might feel if she were to die without him knowing the facts. Week by week she began to gain confidence in taking back control of her own condition, and how she wanted her dad to know. She talked to one of her brothers and between them they found a way for her to spend time with her parents and to talk to them about her illness. Mary's distress levels decreased greatly as a result of these conversations and her deciding on what she wanted to happen in very difficult circumstances.

Hopefully you can see from this brief insight into some of the elements of our training courses how we used ordinary ingredients to put across the message that grief is a normal emotion. Talking about death is healthy, essential and not to be feared.

The bereavement service was also able to ask other bereavement organisations to come and offer training to hospice staff and volunteers over the years. We were fortunate enough to gain grants of money specifically to outsource ongoing training for our bereavement team, which was essential for their continual development. We hosted an end-of-life coaching training day which my friend, Claire Pedrick from 3D Coaching, facilitated in liaison with Don Eisenhauer from America, who was working with Claire.

It was slightly nerve-racking hosting such an event for the first time as we needed to ensure the hospice recouped the money it had paid out for the training, as this couldn't be covered by a grant. Many people who attended had never looked at using coaching for those important end-of-life conversations or in bereavement support networks. I totally agree with Don's statement on 3D's website: 'Coaching conversations are a way of caring for people who are dying or grieving which recognises them as the expert on their own experience.'[43]

Claire also regaled the audience by sharing with them our 'knife experience' from years earlier! I went on to complete an online Coaching at End of Life course[44] with Don in May 2016, which I thoroughly enjoyed. About half a dozen people signed up to the course at the same time and we were given different assignments to complete either in pairs or separately over the next three months. It gave me another useful tool to work with people who were grieving.

Honouring death

In the UK we are good at remembering loved ones who have died in war situations, times of conflict and disasters. One or two minutes of silence are respected at sports grounds, railway concourses, on the streets and in most institutions. Hospices, hospitals, crematoriums and some churches offer people the opportunity to remember their loved ones, usually on an annual basis. Some people need a place to physically go to and spend time, either at a graveyard, a garden of remembrance or a larger place, such as the National Memorial Arboretum near Lichfield,

---

[43] www.3dcoaching.com (accessed 15th October 2019).
[44] See coachingatendoflife.com (accessed 14th April 2020).

Stafford. Where loved ones have died in times of war, they may need to travel further afield.

Over the last few years there has been an amazing television programme called *The Repair Shop*. On the surface it can come across as a quaint, gentle programme where broken treasured items and pieces of family history are brought to the repair shop needing to be transformed. As people bring their items in, they share the memories associated with the personal possession with the person who has the skills to repair the item. It's not unusual for me to find myself in tears as I watch and listen to precious stories. One example I recall concerned an elderly gentleman who bought a portable radio with his wife in the fifties, which became a symbol of their love. The radio broke two years after she died. He brought the radio to the repair shop and the team were able to get it working again.[45]

Personally, I felt it was important to take time to remember each person I had worked with either in the day hospice or out in the community when they died. The danger, if I didn't take time to reflect, was a feeling of being on a conveyor belt, and I never wanted to get to a place of death becoming 'matter of fact'. Honouring each person who sadly died was important for me, whether I took their funeral or not. I bought a lovely leather journal to express my feelings about each person I had worked with. It was a small but important gesture.

---

[45] www.bbc.co.uk/programmes/b08l581p (accessed 18th June 2020).

16
An Unexpected Bombshell

I am very grateful to God for the many occasions in my life when He has graciously prepared me for difficult times ahead. About two and a half years ago I began to experience a tremor in my right hand which I initially thought was related to carpal tunnel syndrome. I didn't pay much attention to it for a while and people were unaware of the problem, as I was able to put my hand in a pocket. When the tremor started to increase a little more, I briefly mentioned it to my line manager but again didn't take it any further. It was only when I took note of other symptoms that were impacting on my well-being that I went to see a GP.

I was struggling to remember people's names and to find the right words when talking or writing, which as a chaplain wasn't ideal! I felt physically exhausted as the tremor in my right hand started to cause a high degree of pain and discomfort and was affecting my ability to focus on work as well as I had been doing. My sleep patterns were all over the place; I was often awake for two or three hours in the night. I was noticeably not as mentally acute as usual. I had numbness down the right-hand side of my upper leg and my balance was impacted if I did too much physical activity. Writing was proving difficult when my right hand was playing up and I had to start using a computer mouse in my left hand.

My hand tremor could kick off on any given day, no matter what I did or didn't do. Sitting on a hard chair would cause major reactions; walking could also bring about an increase in the tremor. I would find that gardening often provoked a physical reaction afterwards. The GP referred me to a neurologist and, while I was waiting for the appointment to come through, I went on an IGR which was already booked in my diary.

During that retreat I sensed God strengthening me for what was ahead, and over the next few months as I underwent tests, I felt quite calm and matter of fact. I was not surprised when the diagnosis came through that I had Parkinson's disease. I had purposely kept away from doing any research online, but I knew enough from working in the hospice to sense that my tremor and other symptoms were going to be related either to multiple sclerosis or to Parkinson's.

There is always a level of confusion around a diagnosis of Parkinson's and I found myself in that same position. A month down the road of seemingly being diagnosed with the disease, I had to take a step back as there were questions around whether I did have that or something else which may or may not be diagnosable! I knew I needed to be patient, to wait, even though part of me wanted to take control and to make some decisions. However, I had to stay in the unknown, remain calm and hold on to the promises of not being alone. Whatever was or wasn't ahead of me was already known by God. He would equip and strengthen me despite the physical and mental frailties.

The neurologist wanted to clear up any confusion concerning the diagnosis, and the only way that could happen was to have a special DaTscan (a scan to detect abnormalities in the brain). Because this was such an expensive procedure, the consultant had to make the referral to a medical panel who would make the ultimate decision whether I could have the scan! I must admit I wasn't impressed with the prospect of being turned down for an incredibly important test owing to financial limitations. Thankfully, they agreed to the referral and I went ahead with the scan, which confirmed I did have Parkinson's.

The consultant spent some time with me explaining how Parkinson's is a progressive neurological condition and is linked to a chemical named dopamine, contained in the brain. Dopamine acts as a messenger between the parts of the brain and the nervous system that help to control and to coordinate body movements. If these nerve cells die, the amount of dopamine in the brain is reduced. Unfortunately, by the time people are diagnosed with Parkinson's, they have already lost seventy or eighty per cent of their dopamine-producing cells.[46]

Parkinson's manifests itself differently in every person, which makes it incredibly difficult to plan and to make appropriate decisions as it's an unknown pathway. I encountered many patients in the hospice who suffered with Parkinson's and had been doing OK for some time. But within a period of six months they had deteriorated significantly to the point where they were unable to walk unaided and struggled with swallowing and talking. It

[46] www.parkinsons.org.uk (accessed 18th January 2020).

was even more distressing to see the mental deterioration where 'the lights had gone out' inside some people who had the disease.

I found it quite difficult to process all the ramifications concerning my diagnosis, more so as I could not see what was physically going on in my brain! The consultant I saw at the local hospital was very nice but was swamped with patients much further down the line than I was. I was also uncomfortable about meeting patients from the hospice at the hospital. I had contacted the local Parkinson's nurse myself through the hospice, who was equally very nice, but she had more than 600 patients on her books. I sensed the medication I had been put on was not being hugely effective.

In the early days I was constantly 'encouraged' by people who told me they knew folks who had had the disease for ten, twenty years plus, and how they had continued to function very well. So on one level I was aware that, compared to many people, I was in a good place, but it was still very difficult to get my head around such unknowns in terms of acceptance. I downplayed how unwell I was, knowing I was physically better than many others.

There was plenty of opportunity to read a huge amount about the disease from the Parkinson's UK website if I so desired. However, I was cautious about doing this for fear of being overwhelmed and scared by acquiring information concerning what may or may not happen in the future. During this time someone kindly reminded me that, as an ordained Church of England priest, I could be referred to London to see someone privately through the charity St Luke's Hospital for the Clergy. The charity used to be linked in to the hospital but that has now closed; instead it links people up with the consultant they need to see.[47]

I asked my GP to refer me to the charity, but as there was a lengthy waiting list I decided to pay for the initial meeting myself. While I waited for my appointment, I decided to take a month off work to see if some time out would help my level of exhaustion. At this stage I was about a year away from when I had first sensed something wasn't right.

I spent the first week on retreat, which enabled me to start facing how much I had tried to run away from the Parkinson's label and from what it was already doing to my body and mind. I was utterly unimpressed at not being able to ignore the disease! I recognised the past year had been a bewildering mixture of ignoring, fighting, adjusting, 'giving in' to the lethargy and exhaustion and generally feeling like being in a fog. In among all of that, I had been doing my level best to keep on top of a demanding job and coping with some people who were expecting me to be managing perfectly well. They were then taken aback when occasionally I became slightly grizzly!

My time out quickly came to an end and I returned to work. I was disappointed at not feeling rejuvenated from my month off, but in hindsight four weeks was never going to be long enough to see vast improvements.

I had recently undertaken a ten-week 'Parkinson's Warrior' specialist exercise programme which was held at the local hospital. Its main aims were to improve balance,

---

[47] www.stlukesforclergy.org.uk (accessed 18th January 2020).

coordination, stiffness and flexibility. It was very useful in helping me to understand the importance of keeping physically mobile as much as possible and the value of working on some of the cognitive deficiencies I recognised I was already experiencing.

It was a huge relief to be seen privately by a neurologist at the National Hospital for Neurology and Neurosurgery based at Queen Square, London, who specialised in Parkinson's. He was (and still is) delightful. Sue came with me to the appointment, and to subsequent ones, as I acknowledged I might not be able to remember all the details of the consultation. The neurologist changed my medication, which had an immediate beneficial physical impact as my hand no longer tremored, my sleep pattern improved and I had more energy. He offered to continue to see me and transferred me to his National Health clinic, which I gratefully accepted.

Unfortunately, a few months later, I suffered an allergic reaction to the new drugs, which I had been warned might occur, but it was still disappointing when it happened. I was afraid I would have to come off the drugs if the side effects persisted, so held back from seeing a GP for a few months. When I finally accepted the side effects were not going to go away, I reluctantly went to see a GP. However, because I was now being treated at a London hospital, they stated they were unable to help and suggested I contact the local Parkinson's nurse who in turn said I needed to talk to the consultant. It was a frustrating process to go through, and even when the consultant wrote a strong letter to the surgery I was attending, I had to keep battling for a change to the medication. In the end I took the decision to come off the drugs altogether as the side effects were having a major impact on my general well-being.

Eventually I was swapped to a slightly lower regime of medication, which was still better than the drugs I had been prescribed at the onset of my diagnosis. Thankfully there were no side effects with the new regime. I also asked to see the senior GP at the surgery and explained my frustration and disappointment at the fiasco I had recently gone through. He understood my concerns and made a note on my medical file that I was to see him if I needed to at any time.

Losing my hand tremor was fantastic, but it gave me a false sense of, 'I am OK now and I can do what I used to do.' Not having any physical outward symptoms, which of course I was grateful for, meant the disease was now more masked. This made the acceptance process more difficult as I had to again make adjustments from the drug regime improvements.

Another reason for wishing to be under a London hospital was based around the area of research. I didn't want to be in a situation further down the line when someone informed me that I could have been part of a research programme if I had been in the right place! There is a huge amount of ongoing research in trying to find a cure for Parkinson's, and if at any point in the future I am asked to be part of a project, I would gladly consider agreeing to sign up.

Sue encouraged me to contact one of her friends who had lived with Parkinson's for several years and gave me his email address. It took me a while to contact him as it signified another step forward in accepting the disease. However, it was extremely useful talking to him via email as he was the first person I talked to who had the disease. It enabled me to ask him more detailed questions, and he in turn encouraged me to attend a First Steps course which was regularly held in Witney, Oxfordshire, over two separate days.[48]

The course was aimed at people who had been diagnosed during the past year, and the organiser worked hard at putting similar-aged individuals together. It covered many practical and emotional issues of living with Parkinson's with the strong message that there is life after a diagnosis, and you can manage your symptoms and live life to the full. It was a helpful workshop and I came away a little further on in accepting the condition and acknowledged the importance of keeping mobile and physically active. Regular exercise, preferably via a Parkinson's group, using relaxation techniques and going to a dance class were all encouraged.

One of the things I have struggled with is having to take regular medication. This may sound strange, as I know the drugs are aimed at controlling the disease and keeping it at bay for as long as possible. It was difficult at work to take my tablets at the correct times with my days being so full, and I resisted setting an alarm as a reminder. I decided to buy some coloured capsule containers for each day of the week's tablets to avoid feeling I had to conform to being 'ill', which has helped in a small way.

I have also had to be careful not to look ahead, as it can feel overwhelming. There is no cure for Parkinson's disease, and many people are only mildly affected and

---

[48] https://localsupport.parkinsons.org.uk/activity/first-steps-oxfordshire (accessed 20th May 2020).

need no treatment for several years after their initial diagnosis. However, the disease is chronic and progressive, meaning its symptoms grow worse over time. Knowing it is highly likely that I will die from Parkinson's disease and my brain cells are dying more quickly than they should be isn't a pleasant prospect. As a single person, I want to be able to make the correct decisions at the right time as to when to downsize in terms of my living accommodation and where best to be when I may not be able to look after myself. In all of this, of course, I hold on to my faith and my relationship with God, knowing He fully understands my fears and uncertainties.

I had asked the consultant at my local hospital what the likely impact of Parkinson's would have on the job I was doing at the hospice, but she hadn't been able to answer my concern. When I saw the consultant in London, I put the same question to him, and this time got a very definitive reply. He did not hesitate to say that if I were to continue in the line of work I was undertaking at the hospice, my deterioration would be accelerated. I had some serious thinking and praying to do; there was no point asking the question if I didn't take the answer my consultant had given me to heart. My health needed to take priority over everything else. I took considerable time to weigh up all the different factors involved in my decision-making.

I spent several sessions with my spiritual director talking through how I was feeling about having Parkinson's. I needed to ask an important question that had been going around and around in my mind as to whether the onset of Parkinson's was a consequence of the physical and emotional abuse I had suffered as a child. I had gleaned from reading about the disease that stressful life events may damage the dopamine cells in our brains. I knew, even as I aired this extremely difficult question, that only God would know for definite and it was essential I laid these thoughts out before Him, as it was too heavy an emotional and mental burden to carry. I also recognised the dangers of the lurking emotions of feeling like a cast-off, abandoned and being of no use any more.

I sensed God say to me in reply to these fears that I was being reshaped, refined, and it would take time for me to see the end product. It was important to focus on who I am inside and not on the outside appearance. The depth, the height, the width of the inner vessel I was being reshaped into being was far, far more important. I was not being discarded. During one of my sessions with my spiritual director I wrote down what I believed God said:

> Child, I want you to come even deeper with Me, to experience that total dependency on Me, to hold on to these daily promises of hope, faith, joy and peace. Your hope in Me will not be thwarted; your faith in Me will not be dashed; your joy in Me will be a delight to you; your peace in Me will be constant. As your physical strength lessens, the spiritual strength which I offer you will grow even stronger. As I dress you in these profound inner gifts, stay close to My heart. Take this step of letting go, of becoming even more dependent and vulnerable in me. I will not hurt or betray you. My love is perfect and is perfect even in suffering.

My director encouraged me to spend time looking at and meditating on some verses from Psalm 63:

You, God, are my God,
earnestly I seek you;
I thirst for you,
my whole being longs for you,
in a dry and parched land
where there is no water.
I have seen you in the sanctuary
and beheld your power and your glory.
Because your love is better than life,
my lips will glorify you.
I will praise you as long as I live,
and in your name I will lift up my hands.
I will be satisfied as with the richest of foods;
with singing lips my mouth will praise you.
On my bed I remember you;
I think of you through the watches of the night.
Because you are my help,
I sing in the shadow of your wings.
I cling to you;
your right hand upholds me.
(Psalm 63:1-8)

I made a covenant with my heavenly Father and my spiritual director that I would not allow Parkinson's to take over my inner being.

17
Adjustments and Another Setback

After spending time considering the advice my hospital consultant in London had given me, including praying and talking it through with people who loved me, I decided I needed to resign my role at the hospice. There were several factors behind my decision. As a chaplain I was struggling with seeing Parkinson's patients in the day unit. I didn't want to notice the levels of deterioration they were going through and the possible likelihood of being in their shoes sometime in the future. I was also constantly surrounded by people who were devastated by a loved one who had sadly died, some of whom had suffered with Parkinson's.

I had attended a day's workshop in London in connection with the grant the bereavement service had received, which was being managed by Hospice UK. I mentally struggled to achieve what was being asked of me during the different exercises. It took until the evening to recognise that the side of my brain being affected by Parkinson's had caused the stumbling block and it sent me on a downward spiral emotionally and mentally, which took a while to pick myself up from.

I felt I was no longer able to pull my weight as a member of the senior management team; all my energy levels were focused on maintaining the bereavement service. I sensed most of the other members of the senior team were struggling with the changes they were seeing. They were so used to me undertaking the supportive role. I had withdrawn into myself and they didn't really know what to say, what not to say or do. None of those dynamics were proving conducive to managing my Parkinson's well.

Given the uncertain nature of Parkinson's, I felt that if I had another five 'good' years left of my working life (which was a pure guess), then it was an appropriate time to make a move. I aimed to look for a part-time job and to look at downsizing in terms of accommodation. I wanted to be able to accomplish both while I had the necessary physical and mental energy.

Making the decision was one thing, but I was walking away from the hospice with a heavy heart – leaving what I considered to have been the best role I had been privileged to carry out. Working the three months' notice was incredibly stressful but I prioritised ensuring my wonderful and amazing team of staff and volunteers were as prepared as they could be. At the end of November 2018, I left the hospice.

It has been essential to take considerable time to grieve my losses at having to give up my vocation and the physical impact the disease is already having on my body and mind. Thankfully, that winter was incredibly mild and I was able to spend a huge amount of time renovating my garden. It was very therapeutic on many levels and I enjoyed spending quality time outside. I also appreciated having an increased social life as I had more time to meet up with family and friends. Starting to write has equally been a useful distraction. I kept my eye out for any suitable part-time job, but so far no door has opened. Attending my weekly Parkinson's exercise class and doing as much gardening as the weather permitted were priorities in the diary, as well as volunteering a day a week for a local counselling organisation where I assisted with some administration tasks.

The emphasis then moved on to the question of where God was leading me to next. When I saw my 'dream job' being advertised to join the team at Penhurst Retreat Centre, near Battle, where I had attended for many retreats, I was mega excited. Two posts were on offer and I knew which one I would prefer. I filled in the application form and was shortlisted for an interview. I spent a considerable time praying about the job and knew that it was a full-time post in a busy environment. I was asked to look at both roles and, as I spent time perusing the different positions, I started to feel some disquiet. However, it felt right to continue with the process and Sue offered to help with the driving. We booked into a local bed and breakfast place for the weekend, as the interview was scheduled for most of the Saturday.

It was very useful having Sue accompanying me, as her initial reaction on seeing the retreat centre before the interview was one of shock at its geographical remoteness. I hadn't given that any thought as it was one of the reasons why I valued going there. On the day of the interview I was somewhat perturbed by feeling incredibly flat; there wasn't an ounce of excitement in me. I was very laid back during all the interviews, which went on throughout the day. The most important session was spending time with the present managers of the centre, whom I had got to know slightly during the times I had been on retreat. My questions to them were all based around whether I could physically cope with a full-time role on top of managing my Parkinson's and being a single person.

They expressed their concerns around the remoteness of the centre and shared how there were times when it would be cut off during snowfalls in the winter and the unreliability of the local train service. They feared a single person might feel incredibly isolated at certain times of the year. The interviews ended and the candidates were informed it would be a few days before we would be contacted concerning the outcome.

Travelling back home the next day, I shared with Sue how I wouldn't know what my decision would be if I were to be offered one of the two roles. I went on to say that I hoped the choice would be made for me by the interview panel turning me down. I concluded that wasn't helpful to the interviewers and emailed them to say I was withdrawing from the process. It felt wrong to wait in case I was offered one of the two roles and to then decline it. People were astonished on hearing my decision to withdraw, but when I explained the different factors to them, they agreed with my conclusion.

I don't regret putting myself through the application and interview process; I had gone into it with the prayer, 'Close the door, Lord, if this is not right,' firmly in the centre of my mind. I would have always wondered whether I should have applied for the role if I hadn't gone for the job. I was, of course, sad to let go of the amazing opportunity, but it was another reminder of the importance of putting my physical needs first.

Moving forward to August and I was back in London with Sue to see my hospital consultant. Unfortunately, I had to bring my follow-up appointment forward as I had been struggling with new physical symptoms. Since May I had started to experience facial nerve pain, which I assumed was another indicator of my Parkinson's. My consultant said unfortunately it was something separate and diagnosed trigeminal neuralgia. The trigeminal nerve can be found inside the skull and pain is caused when a nearby blood vessel presses on part of the nerve.

Initially, pain was provoked when I cleaned my teeth, put a jumper on, dried my hair or gave someone a hug. Once I had worked out what aggravated the pain, I was able to manage the attacks. The pain then disappeared for a few weeks. Unfortunately, it returned and with a vengeance, which I discovered is the typical structure of this condition. This time there was no pattern to the onset of pain; it could happen when I was talking, eating, being outside on a windy day or with any bodily movement. The pain was like an electric shock and was unpleasant and scary. Like most people these days I made the mistake of looking up the definition of trigeminal neuralgia on the internet and groaned. I wished I hadn't, as what I read was not good! Appropriate painkillers joined my other regular medication.

As Sue and I walked back to the railway station to catch our respective trains home, we were talking about the process of writing this book, as I had asked her to read a draft version for me. I shared how much I have valued and appreciated the opportunity God has given me to write about my personal experiences.

Humanly speaking, I could look back over this period and mourn the number of things I have 'lost'. My vocation, my health and my income have all been severely diminished. However, the joy of taking the time to write about my life story alongside the value of going on retreats has been a healthy distraction, rather than focusing on the losses.

18
Shocking News

During the last few meetings when I met up with my spiritual director, there was a clear sense of being prepared for something new. I assumed it would be related to my health, but how wrong I was shortly proved to be!

Sue and I tried to spend a day together about every six weeks. She would travel up by train and we would enjoy catching up and having fun. The Saturday in mid-September was one of those occasions and we had a fabulous day together. We had breakfast, then decided to go to a second-hand bookshop which was based on a farm and had a good reputation. The bookshop took you on an exploratory journey around corridors and corners, and you didn't know what you were going to find at each junction. There was an array of armchairs around the place to sit and browse; there was even a log fire right at the end of the shop!

There were small outlets which had loads of antique goods in them and an incredible coffee shop with mouth-watering cakes. The coffee shop was literally surrounded by a plethora of plaques and humorous knick-knacks. You could spend hours just looking and enjoying the whole atmosphere, as well as working out how many books you could possibly take home with you!

We took advantage of the country lanes situated around the bookshop and had gone prepared to pick blackberries. It was, after all, a good way to use up some of those cake calories we had consumed over our lunch! We filled our containers to the brim and then went back to my house for a well-earned cuppa. We spent the rest of our time chatting and I shared how I wanted us to plan something to celebrate my sixtieth birthday as circumstances had not allowed us to do anything earlier in the year. We both agreed to start thinking about a special holiday next year. It was then time for Sue to catch her train back to Watford; we had had a special day together.

On the Sunday, Sue preached in the morning at both the churches she was involved in and chilled out in the afternoon. I received a phone call from her at about half-past six that Sunday night where she said she didn't want to worry me but she had had to call an ambulance. She was in a lot of pain and was struggling to breathe. I could tell by her voice she was in a lot of discomfort.

After several hours at her local hospital, Sue was blue-lighted to Hammersmith Hospital in London, and at that stage she was in a coma. She had suffered an aortic dissection of the heart and was in Intensive Care. I spent the Sunday night praying alongside receiving and replying to texts from Sue's daughter. I attempted to barter with God, saying I was very willing to take Sue's place. After all, Sue had a husband, children and grandchildren who needed her. I sensed God gently nudge me to let go of the bartering and to place Sue in His hands.

Incredibly, Sue woke from her coma during the Monday and her family were able to spend quality time with her (I believe that was a precious gift from God). Unfortunately, she had suffered a slight stroke at the same time as the major bleed to her heart. That meant the hospital were reluctant to operate, as they felt it was too dangerous. Sue seemed to be in remarkable spirits; she told a doctor that he could stop worrying about her. She made her family laugh and she asked if they had kept in touch with me! The family were encouraged to go home to get some sleep that Monday night as Sue was deemed to be in a more stable place.

Sue's daughter rang the hospital ward early the next morning to see how her mum had been during the night. The nurse who answered the call handed the telephone to Sue and they were able to have a great chat together. However, as the family were on their way into London, they received a phone call from the hospital to say she had deteriorated; half an hour later, Sue had died from another bleed.

There are no adequate words to explain the sense of utter shock and heartbreak at Sue's death. All the usual feelings kicked in for the family, and for all who loved her, of grief, disbelief, anger, numbness and denial over the ensuing days. Her husband and two children organised Sue's funeral and asked me if I wanted to say something at the service. I said I wanted to share a tribute to Sue even though I knew how incredibly difficult that was likely to be.

Someone recently described grief as a black hole, and I think they are spot on. He went on to say the only thing that makes the black hole tolerable is the memories we take with us into that place of pain. I reckon those memories bring glimmers of light to help us to hold on to hope and to take a day, or half a day, or even an hour at a time when another wave of grief attempts to emotionally poleaxe us.

A week before the funeral, my body had a major allergic reaction to the painkillers I had been prescribed for the trigeminal neuralgia and I had to come off the tablets. At this stage I had little voice, but thankfully the pain seemed to be in remission, as I needed to let my body recover from the allergy before starting on some new painkillers. I was also grateful that I had managed to compile most of the tribute to Sue before this latest physical setback.

Four hundred people attended the crematorium and church service for Sue, which was amazing. That factor alone demonstrated how this incredible lady had touched so many people's lives over the years. I had the honour and privilege of knowing Sue for seventeen years. She was a gentle-natured lady, she was incredibly patient, showed great depths of unconditional compassionate love, always gave her undivided attention, listened intently, was a great encourager and supported many people implicitly. She had an infectious smile and a great sense of humour.

I have shed more tears over Sue's death than at any other time in my life. My life has been so much richer for knowing and loving her as a friend and soulmate. When we were both learning the ropes of preparing and preaching sermons, we would email them to each other and ask for honest feedback. We would text each other constantly throughout the day, just sharing the normal stuff of life. It was a real joy seeing Sue gain in confidence in her role as a Reader and as she took on other leadership roles within her diocese. She had literally just finished writing a sermon she was hoping to preach in the churches in her area to encourage others to look at becoming a Reader.

I have spent years supporting a vast multitude of people who have been living with grief. I knew God had given me gifts of being empathetic, of listening deeply and of offering hope in each of those encounters. I now realise that without personally going through a major bereavement myself, it was only possible to go so far in my understanding of grief. Sue's death has well and truly changed that.

It is vital that I cling on to the promises I received during the last spiritual direction session I had before Sue's death, which included some paraphrased words from Isaiah 42:3:

> Do not fight this darkness in your own strength. Come to Me, rely on Me, lean on Me. I will not break the bruised reed; I will not snuff out the smouldering wick. My breath of life restores you.

The stark reality is I now need to wait, to take time to grieve, to be gentle and patient with myself, and to literally take one day at a time.

19
Conclusion

More than forty years of walking with God deserves an almighty celebration, and writing this book has been an apt way of doing that. It feels a privilege to have been given the opportunity to look back over my life and to charter the journey I have undertaken.

There is an incredible contrast in what my life was like before coming to faith compared to who I am today. God has taken a very damaged young adult and has weaved depths of His intimate and compassionate love into the depths of my being. The transformation is awesome, and I am utterly astonished and truly grateful.

It is a joy to see how God has interwoven His plans for me throughout my working life. I echo those words God proclaimed to the prophet Jeremiah: 'For I know the plans I have for you ... plans to prosper you and not to harm you, plans to give you hope and a future' (Jeremiah 29:11). Each of my jobs has linked in to the next stage, has lovingly been prepared by God and has been highly significant in the overall calling on my life. If anyone had said to me on escaping my parents' clutches as a naïve, damaged eighteen-year-old that I would become an ordained priest serving God in a hospice, I would have dismissed their words as nonsense.

I have been asked if those early childhood experiences had an impact on the life choices I have made. Without doubt, those years of abuse, isolation and imprisonment profoundly shaped my personality. Have I regretted making those vows as a young adult not to marry and consequently not to have children? I can't say I haven't. I know God has done an incredible redemptive work within me which could have incorporated my being married and enjoying the delights of motherhood. I equally know how much God has been able to use my singleness in a positive way through the work He called and equipped me to. I have wondered and feared whether my level of physical and emotional intelligence was detrimentally impacted by the lack of healthy childhood developmental stages. Again, I believe God has supernaturally overridden those deficits as I have developed a great level of self-awareness, empathy, motivation and self-regulation, which are some of the key features of emotional intelligence.

I value spending quality time on my own; I struggle to be in large groups so find environments such as church or other large institutions deeply uncomfortable at times. I am predominantly an introvert, can be quite shy with social occasions but also have extrovert strands to my nature when I am in a training environment. I thrive being on the fringes, looking for and supporting people who are not being welcomed or included. I resist conformity, not from a sense of rebelling, but out of a belief that we are all individuals and there is so much richness and diversity in thinking outside the box. I fundamentally believe in being part of a team and enabling others to grow in confidence.

Because I know how miraculously God has worked in my life, I have a simplicity (which I accept could be regarded as naïve) in expecting the impossible to happen. I take great pleasure in focusing on the simple everyday things of being, and hope I will never, ever settle for mediocrity or second best.

Intermingled with my life story, I have shared how God has produced a wealth of spiritual strength and resilience in me that I wouldn't have thought humanly possible. My earthly parents inflicted a legacy on me which on every level was dysfunctional and flawed. My heavenly Father's legacy has and continues to be the very opposite. We have an incredible God who can and does transform darkness into light, hatred into love, emptiness into fullness, abandonment into adoption, poverty into richness, scars into treasure, beggar's clothes into royal robes, shame into acceptance and death into life.

There are no magic wands in God's ongoing transformation in our lives. He expects and waits for His children to play their part in a desire to want to know Him more and to invite Him continually into those more damaged and shadow parts of our being.

Alongside those gifts of being called, love, forgiveness, relationship, adoption, belonging, restoration, life and the gift of clothing which I believe I have received from God in the place of banquet, He has spoken many wondrous words into my inner being. I would like to share two of those occasions as a testimony to His healing, unconditional love:

Child, from the very moment of your conception I have loved you and I have never, ever stopped loving you. My love has beaten death, where humans tried to end your life; my love was there, holding you, sustaining you. My love is an eternal flame beyond your wildest imagination and cannot be drowned out. My love will never, ever run dry. As you go from here know you don't leave Me; come to the banquet table, come to the garden, eat, drink, discover and, above all, love. All that you need is here.

[This encounter took place on one of my retreats in 2017.]

There is no more darkness for you, child, from all that went on in your childhood and early adult life. Out of all that darkness has come My light. Out of all those shadows of death there are now sunbursts of life. I have shattered the yoke that has burdened you, child, and have shattered the bar that has been across your shoulders.

[2019 from a session with my spiritual director.]

I share these with the prayer that people reading this book will be encouraged to find their own ways of discovering the gifts God has waiting for them in the spectacular place of the banquet hall. I am very mindful of the dangers of expecting these mountaintop experiences that can happen when going on a retreat to become the 'norm', which isn't sustainable or healthy. However, as you have read, my life has not stayed at a mountaintop at all – far from it! You know I end this book in a valley of mourning.

One of the recurrent themes that has run through my journey with God can be linked to the verses from the book of Isaiah: 'I will give you hidden treasures, riches stored in secret places, so that you may know that I am the LORD, the God of Israel, who summons you by name'

(Isaiah 45:3). God encourages all His people to seek out those 'treasures hidden in the darkness' (NLT).

I have absolutely no idea what my future holds, where my health will take me or whether God has got another piece of work for me to embark on. What I do know and hold on to with confidence is that in God's eyes I am His precious adopted daughter; I am much loved, and I belong in His precious eternal kingdom.

God invites all His children to His banquet hall and delights to demonstrate His extravagant love by spending quality time with each of us individually. He knows, as His children spend time with Him in this place of banquet, what their unique needs are and lovingly bestows significant gifts upon us. These gifts enable us to go even deeper in our relationship with *Abba* Father, the Lord Jesus and the Holy Spirit.

I end this part of my journey echoing these powerful words from the apostle Paul:

> Now to him who is able to do immeasurably more than all we ask or imagine, according to his power that is at work within us, to him be glory in the church and in Christ Jesus throughout all generations, for ever and ever! Amen.
> (Ephesians 3:20-21)

Appendix A
Spiritual Assessment Questionnaire

Family / friends

Who are the important people in your life?

Do you talk about your illness with those closest to you?

Is there any friction between you and your loved ones which you would like to address? Is there anyone with whom you would like to be reconciled?

Planning ahead

Have you made a personal will?

Have you been able to talk with your loved ones about your final wishes, where you wish to be cared for and your funeral plans?

Would you like to leave a personal memory box or something else for your loved ones?

Character

Are you able to hold on to a sense of your own dignity and purpose?

Is there anything that is worrying you or causing you anger at the moment?

What makes you feel most at peace, even for a short time?

What do you hold on to during the difficult times or when you are feeling down?

Religious

Are there any spiritual or religious resources that you draw on? Are you part of a religious or spiritual community?

Has being sick affected your ability to do things that help you spiritually (or affected your relationship with God)?

Are you worried about any conflicts between your beliefs and your medical situation / decisions?

Appendix B
The 'I Matter' Framework
Questionnaire

1. What do you feel are the important qualities to ensure a healthy work balance?

2. What can cause a bad day at work?

3. How do you look after you?

4. Do you feel valued at work?   Yes   No   Unsure

5. What helps you to feel valued?

6. What makes you feel under-valued?

7. How do you maintain a sense of feeling valued?

8. What negative influence can derail the process?

9. What would you do if you did not feel valued in the future?

10. What solutions can you think of to help problem-solve the above negative influences?

11. Are there hidden myths that need dispelling?

12. How can we dispel these myths?